I0070693

DECISION DECADE:
Age 55 *to* 65

DECISION DECADE:
Age 55 *to* 65

A FINANCIAL ROADMAP TO
OUR GOLDEN YEARS

MIKE LOCKWOOD, CFP®

Unstoppable CEO Press

Copyright © 2023 by Mike Lockwood

All rights reserved. No part of this publication may be reproduced, distributed or transmitted in any form or by any means, including photocopying, recording, or other electronic or mechanical methods, without the prior written permission of the publisher, except in the case of brief quotations embodied in critical reviews and certain other noncommercial uses permitted by copyright law. For permission requests, write to the publisher, addressed "Attention: Permissions Coordinator," at the email address below.

Mike Lockwood
Mike.Lockwood@lfg.com
www.lfg.com

Decision Decade, Mike Lockwood — 1st ed. ISBN 978-1-955242-52-3

Foreword

By Celeste Gurulé

Having grown up together in the financial planning business, I was honored and excited when Mike called to ask if I would write the foreword to his book.

There are a lot of books you could read on retirement planning, so why read this book? Throughout the book, Mike shares actual life stories about how he has helped a variety of people with different backgrounds and financial situations successfully navigate retirement planning. You will likely see yourself in one of these situations or relate to one of the individuals highlighted in the book. You will also find that Mike addresses all aspects of retirement so that you will be as well prepared as possible for not only getting to retirement, but through retirement. One of the most important ways to accomplish this is to stress-test your plan which Mike shares in his "what if" approach. Mike writes this book in the same way he communicates and works with his clients, using easy-to-understand language and ideas that have solved real-life problems for real people.

While Mike and I started with the same firm 35 years ago, we ended up taking two different paths. Mike stayed the advisor route, and I transitioned to a leadership role within the firm. In my role, I observed and worked with thousands of advisors, giving me the opportunity to see what approaches provide the very best client experience and have the most meaningful impact. Mike's unique style of caring and seeking to understand all there is to know about a person (not just the numbers but how they think and feel about all things) before building out a comprehensive plan is critical as it greatly enhances the probability that the plan will be implemented and successful. In working with a planner, it is important to understand what they do and don't do as part of their planning process.

Over the years, I have seen the power of planning—and it works! The difference it can make for an individual, their family, and generations to come can be tremendously profound. Financial planning isn't just about investing; it's about what money can do for your confidence, security, and quality of life. As Antoine de Saint-Exupéry said, "A goal without a plan is just a wish." Don't leave your dreams and goals to chance. Take and make the time to work with an advisor and put a plan in place for your future. And the earlier the better ☺. As we say often at our firm, "Honest, intelligent effort is always rewarded."

Finally, I have had the great fortune to work with the best of the best in our industry. With the process he has thoughtfully developed, Mike and his 5-star team are at the top of that list. Mike has made a meaningful difference in the lives of thousands of individuals and families. And now thanks to this book, he can be of help to you too. So proceed with enthusiasm and confidence. You are in good hands here.

Acknowledgments

For several years, I had wanted to document the foundational principles and practices that my team uses for retirement and financial planning, yet something else always seemed to be more pressing. In 2022, though, I decided to make this writing project a priority. A key motivating factor was seeing more and more friends and clients who are completely unprepared for the financial realities of retirement.

So I started writing, and, yes, this book lists only my name as the author. Yet many people worked behind the scenes in some way to help me put these words to paper. I have borrowed ideas and adapted processes that enabled me build my practice and help new advisors to grow theirs. I will in no way be able to thank all of the many individuals who, along the way, helped me grow as a professional, a mentor, and a family man, but I'll do my best.

My wife, Michelle, has been my biggest cheerleader and greatest source of support for the 35+ years she has been in my life. She has always been in my corner silently applauding my success and offering her insight—and she was the person constantly encouraging and pushing me to share my knowledge. Early in my career, during the times we struggled, she may have had more confidence in me than I had myself. Michelle is my best friend, but her best role is being a mom to Nick, Lauren, and Grant.

My mother, Judy, was my first role model. Her ability to just keep putting one foot in front of the other even when things weren't working out in our favor made a lasting impression on me. Her unconditional love for her sons, her determination to survive, and her efforts to create great memories for us never went unnoticed. She consistently tells her three boys how proud she is of us, and we are proud of her and lucky to call her "Mom."

I also want to thank my planning team at Oakwood Wealth Partners: Heather, Terri, Melissa, Burcu, Marisol, Katheryn, Lili, Mike K., Kevin, Marianne, Sean, Valerie, Nick, Matt, and Jaden. We have built—and we continue to build—a team that is the envy of many financial planning practices in the industry. We know that each and every day we must earn the right to serve others. I am very proud of our commitment to the service we provide to our clients, old and new. The way you care not only for our clients, but also for each other warms my heart. I am also thankful for your help on this book, specifically, for offering insight, advice, and the graphics I use to explain my concepts.

This book also wouldn't exist without my clients, past and present. For over 35 years, I have learned as much from you as I hope you have learned from me. I have never taken for granted the opportunity to work with you, to hear your personal stories, and to learn to appreciate what you appreciate. I have known many of you for well over 20 years. I thank you for your continued trust and, most of all, for your friendship.

Also essential to this book are the many mentors in my life, including—in no particular order—Elaine Hoffman, Rex Athan, Ted Santon, Lauren Farasati, Doug Allen, Chuck Goodwin, Paul Cowell, Colleen Bowler, Brandi Stahl, Karl Brantley, Briggs Matsko,

Celeste Gurulê, and Nick Horn. Many mentors at Lincoln National Life have also helped me along the way. To me, a mentor doesn't lead or hover, but instead walks alongside you as you work through the challenges you face. Also adopting the role of cheerleaders, these mentors are glad to have contributed to your growth and take as much pride in your successes as you do. I have had the great pleasure of having many such mentors in my life. Even those who came into my life for a short time left their indelible mark. Other mentors are still with me some 30 or 35 years later coaching me monthly or quarterly. I am grateful to all of you.

I also appreciate the many knowledgeable and experienced members of The Resource Group whom I am proud to consider friends. I had the privilege of serving six years on The Resource Group board with people like Peter Robertson, Craig McIlroy, David Stone, Monte Fitch, and Roberto Duran, to name a few. Since 2001, their willingness to share ideas and time has helped me form the thoughts and processes that guide my planning.

Finally, I want to thank my editor, Lisa Guest. Lisa happened into my life when my son married her daughter. I was not only the recipient of an awesome fourth child, but I gained access to a world-class editor. She took the time to read the manuscript, learn about the retirement planning process, ask questions that needed to be asked, and then ask again. In addition to helping me to keep this book readable, Lisa kept me excited about the process.

And, as a result of this group effort, I am excited to have a book that I hope will enable you to navigate the decision decade and enjoy the golden years of your retirement.

CONTENTS

Introduction

Do you worry—even fear—that you'll never be financially prepared for retirement?

If you're like most Americans, questions like these may be keeping you up at night:

Can I afford to retire?
Do I really have to stay at this job for five more years?
What source of income—if any—will I have when I retire?
How will I pay for healthcare?
What happens to my financial situation if my spouse dies?
When do I turn on Social Security?
Do I need Medicare?
Will I need to pay for a nursing home?
How does life insurance work?
Will I have any money to leave for my kids?

More questions could be added to this list, each one revealing a degree of fear about being financially prepared for retirement.

I know what that fear feels like and looks like. Countless clients have come to me because they don't know if, when, and how they should retire. They, like most people, haven't been taught how to prepare for retirement. That's where—and why—the fear begins: you don't know what to do to protect your financial future.

One of the primary roles of a financial planner who focuses on retirement is to help ease these fears. That, in fact, is the goal of this book: **I want to alleviate at least some of the fear and provide some direction.**

Retirement doesn't have to be scary, and I want to help you plan a smooth transition to the next stage of life when, after decades of grinding away at your career, you can finally enjoy some hard-earned relaxation. You can travel, spend more time with family, learn new hobbies, volunteer in your community, and do anything else you've always wanted to do but haven't had time for during your career years. In retirement, you'll wake up each morning, and your day is yours. All yours.

And these possibilities I just mentioned are only a sample of why retirement is something to anticipate and celebrate, not fear.

But with so many decisions to make between now and then, the prospect of retirement can be daunting.

The key is... *planning*.

If you sit down with a trusted advisor to plan your retirement well in advance, your fear will become confidence. You'll know exactly what to expect when you retire. You'll be able to rest easy knowing you have a plan that not only provides for the good days but also takes into account the many financial bumps in the road you may experience.

In this book, we'll walk through the major financial decisions—and life decisions—that await you, including:

- When to retire
- How to beat inflation with investments
- When to turn on Social Security
- Minimizing taxes in retirement
- Choosing a healthcare plan
- Pension options
- Managing required minimum distributions (RMDs)
- How to replace your paycheck
- How to afford the retirement of your dreams

And more.

If you're ready to start planning how to retire with confidence, read on....

CHAPTER 1

The Decision Decade

What Is the Decision Decade?

The Decision Decade refers to the five years before your retirement date and the five years immediately after the day you retire. These ten years are critical to your retirement planning because many of the decisions you make during this period will be irrevocable. You can't go back and change them; you and your family will have to live with the consequences.

Decisions about Social Security claims, your pension, investments, and your order of depletion, taxes, healthcare, and Medicare truly can impact the rest of your life. These Decision Decade decisions will affect not only you and your spouse or partner, but they could also affect the legacy you leave for your children or heirs.

If you were to ask the average person, "What age are you planning to retire?" most people would say age 65. Why? Because traditionally, pension plans assumed an age 65 retirement, and that's when Social Security and Medicare kicked in. A targeted retirement age of 65 means your Decision Decade spans the time between when you turn 60 and when you turn 70.

However, in the current environment, your retirement age doesn't have to be 65. In fact, our clients consider several possible retirement ages when they sit down with us. Some retire on their own terms at the age they choose. Others have their retirement age chosen for them by an employer or by family circumstances. Different retirement ages will mean people's Decision Decade begins at different times. We're all running on different tracks at different speeds.

Even if you have a retirement date in mind, the Decision Decade is a moving target. It may start a few years earlier or a few years later than you expect. The Decision Decade may not always be exactly ten years either.

Whether you are free to choose the date or the date has chosen you, the sooner you begin planning for your Decision Decade, the more confidently you'll approach those years. My hope is that this book will help you understand and prepare you to make many of those decisions.

If you aren't sure about when to start your Decision Decade, I recommend no later than age 55. That starting point gives you time to become aware of the important decisions you need to make and when you need to make them so that you'll be ready for a healthy retirement. What you learn will also help you with present-day decisions about savings, budget constraints, asset allocation, and more.

Why Is the Decision Decade So Important?

Your Decision Decade is critical to your retirement because many decisions you make during this time are irrevocable. Yes, the stakes are high. So you can't afford to take advice from just anyone, and I strongly advise against trying to make these decisions on your own. Also, don't look around and simply follow in the steps of your neighbor or a co-worker because they're running on a different track, they're running at a different speed, and they'll encounter different speed bumps along the way.

Let's look now at some of the decisions you can't reverse.

When you decide how you're going to take your **pension** (as a lump sum or a lifetime source of income), you can't change that decision two years later. For instance, if you decide to take your pension as a lump sum, you and your spouse will be stuck with that decision and its consequences, good or bad. You might, for instance, struggle initially to manage the lump sum and then, for a very long stretch, struggle with a lack of income. But if you've projected exactly what your income needs are, using your pension as a lifetime source of income could cost your heirs a substantial amount of your assets after you pass. The option you choose will be permanent, so you must understand which option is right for you before you make that commitment.

When you decide to retire and your HR department provides you with your **retirement benefit outlines**, you typically have 30 to 60 days to decide. You might think the option that pays you the highest monthly benefit is the best choice. But what if you were to pass away in three years, not 30? Choosing the highest monthly benefit might mean your spouse wouldn't have that very important income after you pass. If you don't understand these possible scenarios, that monthly income might be reduced substantially when your spouse needs it the most.

Also, for the most part, the decision to turn on your **Social Security** income stream is irrevocable unless you change your mind within the first 12 months after turning it on. If you elect to take Social Security at a younger age, you do so knowing that you will be paid a lower amount each month, but you assume you'll be paid over a longer period of time. If you wait to take Social Security, your monthly benefit will be higher, but you might be paid for fewer years.

The greatest challenge in retirement planning is the reality that we don't know how long you will live, making your Social Security decision even more important. Adding the spousal consideration further complicates this difficult decision.

I'm sure you now see more clearly why you can't be uninformed when you make decisions about retirement. You definitely don't want to gamble your spouse or partner's future on your best guess. Getting informed and learning the ramifications of your decisions will help to prevent future regret.

Another challenge you'll face in the Decision Decade is determining in what **order of depletion** you'll spend your retirement savings. Different types of savings mean different tax consequences. Do you pay income taxes early and take out your tax-qualified money first? Or do you leave tax-qualified money for the end and take out the after-tax money first? Which decision might create a burden for your heirs? If you have enough assets and aren't worried about outliving your savings, do you leave qualified or nonqualified money to your kids? The most recent changes regarding inherited IRAs may impact your answer here. And if you don't have a pension but prefer a consistent fixed income, should you use some of your retirement assets to build your own personal income stream or personal pension plan?

Are you overwhelmed yet? If so, know that you're not alone. Planning for retirement can seem scary, especially if you don't understand finances or don't like trying to figure out how to put together the jigsaw-puzzle pieces of retirement. You are facing high-stakes decisions, but with the right planning, you don't have to fear them. It's the job of a financial advisor to take away this stress and show you the freedom you can experience in retirement. You've worked long and hard for this season of life. Why not reduce the stress as much as you can? A financial advisor can help.

And while we're talking about financial advisors, let me share one more advantage. In August 2022, the investment group Vanguard (Yes...THAT Vanguard) published a study called "Putting a Value on Your Value: Quantifying Vanguard Advisor's Alpha." Seeing that over a 30-year period the average investor in the S&P 500 will earn about 5%, the author suggests that working with a financial advisor over that same period increases your return by 3% (that's an 8% average S&P 500) return. Why the increase in earnings? The advisor, according to the article, will help you with the emotional aspect of retirement planning.

In other words, a financial advisor can calm and reassure investors, convince them *not* to pull out of the equity market in difficult times, and remind them to keep long-term earnings in view. In addition to this psychological aspect of investing, the right financial advisor will also assist in asset allocation, the timing of withdrawals (spending strategy), tax considerations, and rebalancing. The article doesn't mention other obvious advantages of hiring and sustaining a relationship with a financial advisor: a certified financial planner

(CERTIFIED FINANCIAL PLANNER®) can protect the spouse and the heirs by helping with estate and insurance planning.

There are a lot of good reasons to have a CFP® in your corner. Let me introduce you to Mary, who undoubtedly agrees.

The Great Relief vs. The Unending List of What-Ifs

Early in my career, one of my clients was a single woman I'll call Mary. Employed as a lab technician in a hospital, she drove 40 miles each way to work every day. One day I asked Mary, "Why don't you retire?" She told me she didn't think she had enough money—and she was overwhelmed by the idea of finding out whether she did or didn't. Mary also didn't know how to start the financial and retirement planning necessary for her to even consider retiring, so she avoided that planning completely.

During that brief conversation, though, Mary decided to learn where she was financially at the moment, where she thought she needed to be to retire, and what she wanted her retirement to look like. So I walked Mary through the process, first explaining her available income sources and the assets she had accumulated so far. Next, we discussed her current expenses, and then we moved on to projected expenses (including healthcare) and her retirement dreams.

As this discussion got more in-depth, I offered Mary simple explanations and showed her on a big screen my illustrations of the pieces of her personal financial puzzle. I also walked her through all the possible what-if situations she might face—what if taxes went up, what if her Social Security payments were cut, what if her investments dropped in value, etc. We analyzed every financial challenge that could possibly happen. I asked Mary to tell me every worst-case scenario she could think of, and then I showed her how we would deal with it financially.

In the end as she stared at the numbers, she became slightly emotional.

"I *can* retire," she said. "I really didn't think I could."

Now Mary's decision was not "Can I retire?" but "Do I want to retire?" or "When do I want to retire?" **Mary was in complete control of her retirement**. She was even free to consider whether she was ready to retire.

Mary did retire within six months of our meeting, and she took several trips abroad to visit her sisters. Mary had wanted to do that for a long time, but she never thought she'd have the finances to be able to travel like that.

* * * * *

Many people are like Mary. They feel overwhelmed by all the decisions they know they'll have to make. They don't even know where or how to start planning for retirement, and all these unknowns paralyze them. Financial planning might sound stressful—and it can be—but sitting down with the right partner to evaluate where you are now can be the first step into the Decision Decade, the first step toward understanding the retirement process, identifying the various decisions you'll need to make, and analyzing your options. Having a clear picture of where you are today, where you want to be, and how to get there can give you real relief. You'll be able to stop worrying about the what-ifs.

You won't have to fear the future anymore, and you can truly look forward to enjoying the retirement you've earned.

The key is planning. The fact that you're reading this book suggests you're preparing for the Decision Decade when retirement plans take shape. This planning will help you to shut off all the noise that makes people afraid of retirement: the media's talking heads, MSNBC news shows, your neighbors, your co-workers, your siblings, and anyone else telling you what they did and why it's the only way to ensure a successful retirement.

Let me just say, everyone has different ideas about their retirement. We all tolerate risk differently. We each have a unique set of financial assets and our own attitude about saving and carrying debt. We have personal plans for retirement and various pension and Social Security.

These various factors mean that there is not only one way or even a best way to retire. There's just the best way *for you*. You're not running a race against your friends and neighbors. And because everyone's personality and circumstances are unique, you also can't compare your financial plans to other people's. If you do, you'll just start worrying that you're behind and lose sleep.

* * * * *

I was visiting with some old college friends when one of them asked me, "So, Mike, what is The Number?" He wanted to know how much he should save up before retiring.

I told him, "Ryan, there's no such thing as 'The Number.'"

But a lot of numbers are out there. Depending on whom you listen to, you may read that everyone needs $1.7 million to retire, but that's just not true. You might need $800,000. You might need $3 million.

I have clients who can live in retirement on less than $50k a year because they've always lived on $50k a year. Social Security and their small pension cover most of their living expenses. I have other clients, though, who are accustomed to a more affluent lifestyle. They might be willing to adjust their spending habits a bit, but the reality is they'll most likely need their retirement income to come very close to their pre-retirement income. Yet their Social Security will replace a much lower percentage of their pre-retirement income than the first couple's Social Security did. As these two client examples show, "The Number" is different for different couples.

* * * * *

If you start planning early for retirement, you can figure out your number and make any adjustments you need to make. If you start to seriously look at retirement income a mere six months before you retire, then you'll lose sleep—a lot of sleep—because you didn't plan ahead. Again, if you start planning and saving early, you won't be filled with worry. Instead, you'll know the relief of being in good shape or at least the relief of having a plan for remedying your shortfall.

* * * * *

During your working years, you can feel like you're on a hamster wheel, running and running without knowing when you'll be able to get off. If you're a traditionalist about retirement, you've always planned on working until age 65 and then calling it a career. Through good times and bad times, through good bosses and bad bosses, you've muddled through, always trying to live the best life possible until you get to that magic age of 65. And all this time, you're hoping that you and your partner stay healthy enough to enjoy the fruit of your labors.

When you're young, 65 feels far away, and maybe it still does to you. But if 65 is creeping up on you, confusion may set in. You may start wondering if 65 really will be or even can be the end of your career. Or maybe you want to keep working. Or maybe you want to ditch your job as soon as possible, but you don't see how you'll have enough money to pay for the quality of life you want. That's when the target date of 65 that used to get you through tough days at work changes from being a day of freedom to a day of fear. And 65 is approaching faster than you thought it would.

So, again, why not sit down with a trusted and competent financial planner and start the work you know you should be doing? What if you took time now to do some planning and to better understand your options? Imagine comparing your current income and your current expenses to your projected income and projected expenses and looking at your assets as well as your goals... and realizing that you could retire at age 63. What would that discovery do for you? At the very least, you'd have a specific light at the end of the tunnel. You'd know when you can retire, and that *when* is two years *before* you turn 65.

And did you notice the word *can*? No one should tell you when to retire. Just because you *can* retire doesn't mean you have to or should. You want to control that timing. There's power and peace in being able to do so.

If you like your job and decide to stick around a few extra years, you'll go to work each day knowing that if circumstances change (whether at work, in your family, or in your physical health), you have the freedom to retire if you want to.

You are in control, and knowing that will mean more restful nights. You will no longer fear retirement as an end date followed by countless unknowns. You've mapped out your finances with an experienced professional and his or her team, so you can stop stressing about money and instead approach retirement excited about beginning a new chapter of life.

But if you don't have a coach to guide you through the decisions involved in preparing for retirement, you could be losing sleep, taking bad advice from your friends, and/or buying into media myths. You're most likely letting outside forces shape your future when those forces don't know your specific life situation. Case in point.

Too often, new referrals come to me believing that the poor performance of their stock market investments means they have to delay their planned retirement—and hearing them say that is so frustrating for me. People who are making a decision about retirement based on a snapshot of the stock market probably haven't been working with an advisor. You see, financial advisors expect the financial markets to have their periodic down cycles. The role of a competent professional financial advisor is to make sure you will have money correctly positioned no matter how the market is doing, whether we are on an upswing or a downswing.

A financial advisor will tailor your retirement plans to your personal circumstances *and* take into consideration the inevitable fluctuations of the stock market.

* * * * *

Before we move on in our discussion of being financially set for retirement, I want to offer some basic investment education: What are the differences between a stock investment and a bond investment?

In one of my first conversations with my clients, I define *stock* and *bond*. Basically, a stock is partial ownership of a company, and a bond is holding debt to an entity or company. To help this become clearer, I use my ice cream store analogy. In my late high-school years and during my first year of college, I managed the local franchise of a major ice cream chain. Since I have a real-life background in ice cream sales, let's assume I want to open my own ice cream store, and let's assume I need $500,000 to open the store. But only $250,000 of my money is accessible. So I go to you, I pitch to you the idea that I need another $250,000 to open the store, and you want to help. You can help me in one of two ways.

First, you can **invest** your $250,000 with my $250,000, and we open the store as 50/50 partners. In this case, we lease the property, and we buy the ice cream freezers and all the equipment we need to run the store. Then we buy the ice cream and have our grand opening. We do well. We make money hand over fist. And we split the profit 50/50 because we own the business 50/50. Whether we're earning a large monthly amount during the summer or less money in the winter months, we share the profit equally.

But what happens if we don't do so well? Maybe a better ice cream store opens, we hire the wrong management, we can't control our costs, etc. We soon realize we have to close our store after just 12 months. What happens to your investment of $250,000? You lose all of it just as I lose all of mine. We were owners who had **stock** in our own company. Yes, only two shares, but we had ownership and stock.

Now, what if when I ask you for $250,000, you decide to simply **loan** me the money. That loan is a **bond**. So I will promise you that if you loan me $250,000, I will pay you 4% interest on that loan. At the end of an agreed-upon period of time, I will return the total amount of the loan back to you. Your money is currently sitting in cash at the bank, earning 1%, so you believe this ice cream franchise with its return of 4% is a good investment. Remember, you are retired now and looking for income. This investment could help.

When you loan me the money, you essentially become a bank. Fast-forward, I open my store, and I do very well. I earn a lot of money. So how much of that profit do you get? You simply receive the 4% interest on your $250,000 loan that I promised you. You don't share in the profit; you are simply a creditor. But what if I have to close my ice cream store? What happens to your debt? You contact me and tell me to sell the freezers, sell the inventory, sell everything I have so that I can pay back your $250,000. You have a lien of sorts on my business.

Now back to the definitions. Stock is equity: it is partial ownership of a company. When you buy *one* stock in one company, let's say Apple, the entire value of your investment rides on the performance of Apple. But you won't invest in only one company, just as people who might invest in my ice cream store would also have partial ownership of a coffee stand, an air conditioning repair company, a small market, etc. Diversifying your investments among different companies in different industries protects your money: you can't lose everything if one company fails. If, in our example, my ice cream store fails, you have invested in several other companies that are doing well and some that are doing very well. The power of diversification can work for you when you use a platform that can value these companies for you. The same principle of diversification applies to bonds. You will diversify bonds among credit quality, how strong the company's financial statements are, and terms (the length of time between investing in bonds and the point when they reach maturity).

* * * * *

Returning to our discussion of financial preparedness for retirement, let me acknowledge that the Decision Decade can definitely feel overwhelming. After all, you're doing something you've never done before: you're moving from an accumulation mode to a de-accumulation mode. Your finances were pretty straightforward when you were accumulating money: you worked, you tried not to get caught up in the emotional swing of the stock market, and you continued to save money. But now you're entering the de-accumulation mode: you need to be taking money out of savings, but you're unsure where to take it from. You may have no idea how to replace your income. And you may be plenty worried that if you take money from the wrong source, you'll run out of money. That is a real and, I'd say, legitimate fear for many people, especially for people who don't plan.

This fear leads many people—maybe you—to postpone that first appointment with a financial advisor. Maybe you're embarrassed about past financial mistakes. Trust me, we've seen many mistakes; you won't be the first. Or maybe you're not sure what questions to ask. Maybe you're used to handling everything yourself, and you feel awkward or ashamed asking an advisor for help. Perhaps you're afraid you don't have enough money to retire, and you're trying to deny or hide from that fact instead of working as soon as possible to fix it.

Whatever your fears and concerns, you need to take action—and you need to take action now. Please don't kick this essential financial planning work any farther down the road—and definitely don't wait until six months before you retire. If you do, you'll have bigger reasons to be afraid. Legitimately afraid.

Let me reassure you, you're not the first person to be hesitant about looking at the numbers or to have these fears about retirement. What you're thinking and feeling is quite normal. When new referrals come into our office, I often tell them, "I've seen worse, and I've seen better," and it's true. When it comes to financial planning, most people fall right in the middle between those two extremes of worst and best. Again, your financial fears are common. If you've made any financial mistakes in the past, an experienced financial planner knows exactly how to fix them because, after years or even decades in the business, they've seen it all before. I know that because after my 35 years of financial advising, nothing can surprise me.

I can't encourage you enough. Don't let your fears keep you from planning for retirement any longer. The sooner you get busy, the fewer what-ifs will torment you. Get on the path of preparing for retirement. Start planning as soon as possible—before it's too late.

I want you to experience that great sense of relief that comes with knowing you have a secure retirement ahead of you.

CHAPTER 2

Life After Work: Now What?

After the Retirement Party...

Here's a key question for you: Are you retiring *from* or are you retiring *to*? Are you retiring *from* a career, or are you retiring *to* a new phase of life that you're looking forward to?

* * * * *

Picture this. You recently turned 65, and you are at your retirement party, celebrating with a large cake, some balloons, maybe a meal, several speeches, and a few gifts. You've been looking forward to this day for so many years. As you look around, you see all your family, your friends, your co-workers, and other guests. Everyone is celebrating you, your career, and all that you did during your working years to make the people around you better. It really is a great way to mark the milestone. Yet the party means that the future retirement is... now.

The next morning—that first morning of your retirement years— you wake up and start your day in a completely different way than you have for the last 10, 20, 30, or more years. Your normal and longstanding workday wake-up time and morning routine don't quite fit anymore. So maybe you sleep in a little. Today—and every day for the rest of your life—you have a full day ahead of you to do as you wish.

Welcome to your new normal, but what will your new life actually look like? If you don't have a plan for this new season—even a general, somewhat vague plan—you may feel lost. Really lost because the retirement chapter of your life will be a lot different from what you've known. Are you ready for that change?

* * * * *

When I walk new clients through this hypothetical, some of them do have a plan. But most people have no idea what they want to do with their retirement years. Some laugh—nervously. Some offer clichéd answers like "Relax" or "Watch TV," but you can't sit in your underwear and watch Dr. Phil forever….

In an old movie called *About Schmidt*, Jack Nicholson plays a retired insurance executive named Warren Schmidt. After his big retirement party, he goes home, enjoys the weekend, and has a couple of days to himself, but then looks at his wife with an "Is this all there is?" expression on his face. So, one morning a week later, Schmidt wakes up, puts on his tie, and returns to the same office he retired from. He finds the young executive tasked with replacing him and asks, "Is there anything I can do to help? Can I help you find anything?" The young executive politely tells Schmidt he has everything under control as he walks Schmidt to the elevator. Clearly, the company has moved on and filled the retiree's shoes with someone younger. Yes, that stings.

And, of course, it stings. When you've worked for so long, your job feels like your identity, so some (many?) people find it hard to let go. Furthermore, the workplace is often a big part of your social life. You have friends at work: your co-workers are your people. And sometimes going to work has been a break from the harder aspects of your "real life." That was one of the reasons Schmidt ventured into the office a couple of weeks after he retired.

But, again, your career isn't who you are; your career is simply what you did to earn a living. Now you're done with that phase of your life, and you can do whatever you want and be whoever you want to be. Maybe that means doing something simple like volunteering, picking up a fun part-time job, diving into a new hobby, or spending more time on the hobby you've been too busy to enjoy.

Many of my clients decide to continue earning an income. Now that you don't need to earn the income you used to, you can take a lower-paying job doing something you enjoy.

But maybe I'm getting ahead of you. Maybe you're hesitant about retiring because you don't want to leave any work projects unfinished. Remind yourself of the simple truth that there will always be unfinished projects at work. Yet I have clients who put off their retirement for years because they felt they had to see a particular work project through to the end. Or they were afraid of leaving a mess for their co-workers or successor. I understand that sense of responsibility and pride of ownership. But you—like countless others before you—can definitely leave the work projects for someone else and turn your attention to the unfinished projects at home that you've been meaning to get to for a very long time.

Letting go and leaving unfinished work behind is easier when you've made specific plans for this key step of retirement. I compare this big transition to when my children moved out of my home, into their dorm, and started school. I trusted their judgment based on the values their mother and I had instilled and who they were as young humans, but I was seeing them leave their comfort zone. Whether they recognized it themselves, like a plant, they'd outgrown their old pot. Now they had a great opportunity to re-pot themselves and grow.

To that end, we tell our clients, "You need to—and you are going to—re-pot yourself. Your career worked fine for you, but now you need to re-plant yourself in a new pot and find a new challenge. Your career is in the past, and now you can decide what your new normal will be."

What does *your* next phase of life look like? Life won't be the same as before, and that's OK.

* * * * *

Remember, however, yours isn't the only transition happening. Your retirement means a transition time for your spouse or significant other as well. For decades, you left the house for eight hours a day. Maybe they left the house as well; maybe they were always home. Either way, now you're home all the time. Yes, it's great that you have more time to spend together, but you're going to have to navigate the impact of this big change on your relationship. If you haven't already, start to explore activities that you can do together as well as activities each of you will do without the other.

When this topic comes up in financial planning discussions, I sometimes feel a bit like a marriage counselor. Talking about retirement and a couple's new future can bring up issues the two individuals have never discussed.

Also, I often play out scenarios for them to consider: "Joanne, I'm going to talk just to you right now. Tom, you cannot interrupt. So, Joanne, you're now retired. Fast-forward three years, and tell me what life looks like. Do you still live in your current home? In the same state? Are you more involved in clubs... or volunteer work... or your faith? Where do the kids and grandkids live? Is it important to you to be near them? So you have a child living in Texas, one in Idaho, and one in Pennsylvania. How often do you plan to visit them? Have you factored these increased travel expenses into your retirement? Or will you be moving to be near one of the kids? What's your plan?"

Potential retirees sometimes have no idea what fears and insecurities about retirement their spouse has. They may not know what their spouse's wishes and dreams are. I can help them talk through their options until they're both on the same page or at least aligned very closely.

* * * * *

Now that you're retired, you might miss work, and that's pretty normal. Many people miss the social aspect of work: co-workers have often become longtime friends. Now you have to find or create social groups outside of work. Some of my friends, who worked at the same hospital and are either retired or close to being retired, started The Martini Task Force, and they get together regularly to catch up. They were friends before they retired, and they continue to offer each other support after retirement. Another client met a group of men who are now buddies on the golf course, and every Tuesday they have a 6:00 a.m. tee time. You can still have the friends and connections you had at work, but you'll have to be more intentional about staying connected. It's also important to find some new friends, social groups, and even an accountability partner.

Also, before you retired, your work projects kept your mind busy. They gave you an opportunity to use your brain. Now you get to spend that time and mental energy on your own projects and pursuits. Maybe you've always wanted to plan a cross-country trip, discover more about your family tree, learn more about your favorite historical era, or pick up a new language. You can pursue interests that your job forced you to put off. You have more time available for your interests than you've ever had before. Imagine the possible uses of this new freedom!

What Are Your Dreams?

It can be hard to dream about the future when you're so caught up in the demands of the present. And none of us really thinks about bucket list items when retirement feels far away. But when you sit down to plan for retirement and give yourself a chance to think about the future, the idea of retiring can become exciting. Maybe you've dreamed your entire life about a trip to Italy, or maybe a bucket list item is taking annual beach vacations with the grandkids. I have one set of grandparents that choose to take a different grandchild on a vacation each year. They are about creating different memories for each of their grandkids. Putting up a backyard hammock under your favorite oak tree may be on your list. Maybe some of the following questions will help you flesh out your bucket list.

Where will you live? Now that your job isn't tethering you to a certain location, you have the freedom to move if you want to. Maybe you want to be closer to the grandkids, or maybe you've always wanted to live in the mountains. I have one client whose retirement dream was to sell the house, buy an RV, and travel all over the country for a couple of years. Or maybe you want to stay in the same town, but you want to move to a smaller house and cut down on the housework.

Will you travel? Do you have kids who live across the country whom you'd like to visit more often? What dream vacation spots would you like to visit? Will you travel internationally as well as domestically? Once you figure out how much traveling you'd like to do, budget for it in your financial plan.

What hobbies and activities will you participate in? I have clients who do triathlons, play tennis, golf, enjoy bocce ball, and, most recently, are mastering pickleball. Some of my clients have decided to umpire youth baseball games or high school football games. Whatever you like to do, you now have time to do it. Also, as an added benefit, these hobbies often bring you a new social network.

What relationships will you pursue and invest in? As much as you love your spouse, you need to have friends and acquaintances outside of the house. This very necessary social network can come through your hobbies, volunteering, church groups, neighborhood clubs, and other activities.

What Realities Will Impact Retirement?

Give yourself a chance to dream about your ideal retirement future, and then assess the realities of your life and determine how to make that retirement happen. Again, the following questions may help you get a more thorough picture:

Are your parents still alive? Do they live with you? Do you need to live near them? Do you need to pay for their care? Does your spouse have any health concerns that you need to take care of? Have you chosen the timing of your retirement due to the health of your parents, your spouse, or yourself? Does a family member need to move in with you?

What about the kids? Do you need to live near them? Are the kids living with you? Do you need to help them financially? Are you supporting any grandkids financially or otherwise (babysitting, picking up from school, taking them to afterschool activities, etc.)? I have many clients who retire to help with the grandkids.

Will you work in some capacity? Maybe you need to work part-time for a few years to cover healthcare insurance and costs. That's especially likely if you choose to retire before age 65. Will you work to help with the cost of a family member's healthcare? Maybe you simply enjoy working, and that's valid. Maybe you'd like to pick up a part-time job that gets you out of the house as well as provides a little spending money and another social network.

Make sure to consider realities like these when you sit down with a financial advisor. Taking stock of all these factors is critical because they're going to affect what your retirement looks like. If you've always dreamed about living abroad but you need to take care of your elderly parents, you'll want to find a way to balance your dreams and your responsibilities.

The sooner you take some time to dream and determine what you'd like your future to look like—being mindful that any changes in your real-life circumstances may require adjustments in that vision—the easier it will be to make sure your finances support your retirement dreams.

CHAPTER 3

The Paycheck
Replacement Plan

What Is a Paycheck Replacement Plan?

You've been getting paid every two weeks your entire working life. For those 30 or 40 years, your paycheck came in like clockwork. Well, the day you retire, that paycheck stops. What happens then? How will you pay your monthly bills?

Not only did those paychecks arrive regularly, but they were also a predictable amount. You knew how much money you'd have to pay your bills. Again, what happens when you retire? How much money will be coming in—and from where? How will you pay for your retirement dreams?

This is a big issue, but don't be alarmed. When you're working with a financial professional, you'll be able to create your own personal Paycheck Replacement Plan.

Simply put, a Paycheck Replacement Plan is an income stream that functions as your paychecks did. You can arrange to have this income stream pay you monthly or semi-monthly, whatever you were used to when you were working. With this reliable and predictable income stream, you'll be able to pay your rent/ mortgage, utility bills, and car insurance the same way you've been doing it for years. Your transition into retirement doesn't have to mean complicated adjustments or changes. You can work toward the complementary goals of maintaining your current lifestyle, fulfilling your expectations for your retirement years, and making the transition into retirement simple.

And I hope that's great news for you. Many people who come into my office fear that retirement will force them to cut spending. Over time, that might happen, but with your personalized Paycheck Replacement Plan, you can sustain the spending you did and maintain the lifestyle you enjoyed while you were working. You can keep your Wine of the Month Club membership, still go out to dinner with friends, and not have to cancel all your TV subscriptions. You're replacing your paycheck so that as you adjust to retirement, you can keep your budget the same.

After about six months, review your budget and make any adjustments. Initially, you were easing into those adjustments. But now it may be time for some retirement-stage adulting. Obviously, you will make any adjustments only *after* you and your planner have done the projections and any other planning work that needs to be done.

Where Does the Paycheck Replacement Money Come From?

That is the million-dollar question. Where will this stream of retirement money come from? Social Security, pensions, and any investments you've made through the years are some possibilities. You can establish direct deposits from these various income streams just as you did with your paychecks. And you can schedule those deposits from the income streams *that you establish* to come on the same days of the month that your paycheck did. If you pay the mortgage on the first of the month, make sure money is deposited by the 21st of the preceding month, and schedule the other deposit around the 7th to cover utilities, groceries, car payments, etc.

Seeing these self-generated "paychecks" arrive regularly will ease your fear and calm your anxiety. You'll see that you have money to pay the bills like you always did. You won't have to change your bill-paying routine at all.

Establishing your own Paycheck Replacement Plan will protect you from financial headaches and worries about how much money will be coming in and when. Simply put, a Paycheck Replacement Plan will help you enjoy your retirement. But keep reading if you're not yet convinced.

Why You Need a Paycheck Replacement Plan

The first six months of retirement are a scary time of major transition. You're no longer going to work every day, you're wondering what to do with your time, and you're discovering who you are apart from your job. You don't need to add complicated financial changes.

Your goal is simple: at least during the first six months, keep your finances consistent with the income level and rhythm you had while you were working. You have some big issues to think about during this initial transition period, so receiving income from your own retirement savings in the same way that you received payment from your employer and in the same amount you're used to will take a huge weight off your shoulders.

Again, the ideal setup for these first six months is to replace your income in the exact amount and at the same frequency you're used to. Doing so will keep your life as normal as possible while you adjust to retirement. After you've adjusted to this new life of retirement—generally after about six months—you can adjust the income up or down depending on how much you actually need each month.

After all, you knew your spending habits as a working person, but how will these habits change in retirement? Every retiree is different, so we can only guess; you can't really predict the changes retirement brings until you start living it. Maybe you don't need as many nice clothes now as you did going into the office. Maybe you start eating out a little more now that you're retired, or maybe you now have time to cook more at home.

Since you can't predict which of your expenses may change, you'll want to start your Paycheck Replacement Plan in the exact amount of your current paycheck. Then, connect with your financial planner every three to six months during that first year to assess how your spending has changed. Maybe the amount you receive in your Paycheck Replacement Plan isn't enough. More likely, the amount will be more than you need.

Income Flow Chart

One financial planning tool that many advisors use is some version of an income flow chart. In my practice, we use an Excel-based chart after we've completed a full retirement income plan and know the income replacement amount we need. Clients appreciate being able to map out their income for the first five to seven years of retirement.

In addition, after we've entered their Social Security and pension numbers along with any other fixed income amounts (i.e., rental income), the chart puts that income next to inflated expenses. The chart shows us the amount of taxable income before we start layering on other sources of income. The chart also helps us to understand the ratio of taxable income to nontaxable income that we should be considering. We then have a clear illustration of tax-efficient income streams such as Social Security and possible rental income. (This distinction between taxable and nontaxable may be important not only for tax brackets but for possible Medicare surcharge expenses as well, which will be discussed in Chapter 6.)

This income flow chart also illustrates for the client ways we can, if necessary, adjust the faucet by turning income sources up or down or stopping them altogether.

Jack and Jill Johnson
Income Flow Chart (January 2023)

		2022	2023	2024	2025	2026
NON-QUALIFIED						
Trust Account #1		$ -	$ -	$ -	$ -	$ -
	after tax	$ -	$ -	$ -	$ -	$ -
Trust Account #2		$ -	$ -	$ -	$ -	$ -
	after tax	$ -	$ -	$ -	$ -	$ -
Brokerage Trust Account - REITs		$ -	$ -	$ -	$ -	$ -
	after tax	$ -	$ -	$ -	$ -	$ -
TOD Account #1		$ -	$ -	$ -	$ -	$ -
	after tax	$ -	$ -	$ -	$ -	$ -
Savings Accounts		$ -	$ -	$ -	$ -	$ -
	after tax	$ -	$ -	$ -	$ -	$ -
QUALIFIED						
Beneficiary IRA - Jill		$ -	$ -	$ -	$ -	$ -
	after tax	$ -	$ -	$ -	$ -	$ -
Traditional IRA - Jill		$ -	$ -	$ -	$ -	$ -
	after tax	$ -	$ -	$ -	$ -	$ -
Traditional IRA #1 - Jack		$ -	$ -	$ -	$ -	$ -
	after tax	$ -	$ -	$ -	$ -	$ -
Traditional IRA #2 - Jack		$ -	$ -	$ -	$ -	$ -
	after tax	$ -	$ -	$ -	$ -	$ -
Traditional IRA #3 - Jack		$ -	$ -	$ -	$ -	$ -
	after tax	$ -	$ -	$ -	$ -	$ -
Roth IRA - Jill		$ -	$ -	$ -	$ -	$ -
	after tax	$ -	$ -	$ -	$ -	$ -
Inherited Roth IRA - Jack		$ -	$ -	$ -	$ -	$ -
	after tax	$ -	$ -	$ -	$ -	$ -
INCOME STREAMS						
Jack Social Security***		$ -	$ -	$ -	$ -	$ -
	after tax	$ -	$ -	$ -	$ -	$ -
Jill Social Security***		$ -	$ -	$ -	$ -	$ -
	after tax	$ -	$ -	$ -	$ -	$ -
Rental Income		$ -	$ -	$ -	$ -	$ -
	after tax	$ -	$ -	$ -	$ -	$ -
Part-Time Work Income - Jill		$ -	$ -	$ -	$ -	$ -
	after tax	$ -	$ -	$ -	$ -	$ -
Total Minimum Monthly Income - GROSS		$ -	$ -	$ -	$ -	$ -
Total Minimum Monthly Income - NET		$ -	$ -	$ -	$ -	$ -
Essential Monthly Expenses		$ -	$ -	$ -	$ -	$ -
Discretionary Monthly Expenses		$ -				
Jack's Age (year end)		65	66	67	68	69
Jill's Age (year end)		61	62	63	64	65

Adjusting the Faucet

When you retire, you're going to have some fixed income and some adjustable income. Once you've made some decisions about when to start receiving Social Security and any possible pension options, you'll have an idea of what your fixed retirement income will be. You can then plan your other income streams around that fixed retirement income stream. *Determining that amount of fixed income* is important: these are truly a couple of your first *irrevocable decisions.* Know that you will not be able to adjust how much money you get each month once that fixed income amount is set. This amount will always be your base income.

You may, however, have additional sources of income for a finite period of time. Adding this information to the Income Flow Chart offers you a visual of those sources of income that you can adjust, and it's your financial planning partner's job to help you manage those. Your adjustable income works like a faucet. You can adjust the flow—you can turn the water up or down—until you find the perfect amount for you.

You might be wondering why you would ever want to turn down an income stream, and the reason is taxes. Your goal is to both minimize the amount of taxable income you have coming in and make sure your money lasts your lifetime. All of us want to run out of life before we run out of income. If you need the money, you can give yourself more each month, but if you're not using all the money that's coming in, you don't want to unnecessarily be paying taxes on this excess income.

Likewise, if you think you want to turn up your adjustable income, make sure you can afford to do that. If you're spending more per month than you were when you were working, you might be depleting your long-term retirement money. If you and your spouse retire at 65, chances are very good that you will need at least 25 years of income.

Based on how you've lived during your working years and the money you're used to spending, you and your financial planner can project how your spending patterns will play out over 15 to 25 years of retirement. Doing this kind of reality check will show you in black and white whether you can sustain your current rate of spending. Numbers don't lie.

If the numbers show that you can't afford to keep spending at the current pace, realize that what you're doing is like putting money on a credit card that you can't pay off. That never works out well. Simply put, you need to live within your means. Sometimes clients need to hear the cold hard truth that they're spending too much. They may not be happy to hear it, but they will thank their advisor in the long run for keeping them from depleting their retirement money too soon.

I know you don't want to be nagged about your spending habits during your retirement years, but you do need to understand the big picture. A good financial advisor will not only tell you when that picture is rosy but also when you need to make some tough adjustments. Of course unexpected expenses come up—maybe you need to replace a roof, maybe you decide to take the family on a cruise—and that's OK. Your financial advisor's job is to make sure you will still have enough money in savings to last the rest of your life.

* * * * *

Now for some good news. Financial advisors have looked at actual people's spending habits and seen that those spending habits change over time. In fact, we have come to recognize three stages of retirement: the Go-Go years, the Slow-Go years, and the No-Go years.

The idea here is that early in retirement, we are as young and probably as healthy as we'll ever be going forward. In these Go-Go years, we have an easier time getting around, we exercise regularly, and we can take active vacations. As we age, healthcare costs begin to increase, but our travel expenses will start slowing down. Instead of taking a trip to Europe, we stay in the States. We visit the grandchildren and stay in a modest hotel. These are the Slow-Go years. Then, as we age into the No-Go years, the only travel we do is to see our doctor.

We can make light of this, but the point is, our spending habits do change as we age. You won't always spend money the way you're spending it now. It makes sense that you'll have a bigger monthly budget when you're younger, active, and able to do more things. You and a financial advisor just need to make sure you have enough money to live comfortably during your Slow-Go and No-Go years. And it's important to meet regularly to adjust your income plan as your spending patterns change. For the first few years of retirement, though, your income will probably match your working income, so your lifestyle doesn't have to change much, if at all.

*   *   *   *   *

When you consult with your financial advisor, you also want to make sure that you maintain multiple income streams so that all your money isn't coming from one source. For example, people who retire with a 401k that is invested in a traditional lifespan model and has a set investment mix and who use this as their only source of supplemental income may forget about the risk of a sequence of returns (explanation coming). These people may think they're fine, but the amount of income they choose to receive will always change the total asset value based on the annual performance of the underlying investments. Retirees don't have much control over the value of those 401k investments, and the challenge is knowing how much money will be coming in from them if the economy goes through a few years of an unforgiving equity market.

While our 401k income may seem fine when we first retire, we are playing Russian roulette with our income 15 years from now. Let's assume, for instance, that you believe your assets will grow at an average of 6% per year and that you can withdraw 5% per year and do just fine. First, invested assets may *average* that given 6%, but the range it can fluctuate may be extreme. One year, we can be up quite a bit or just a little, and the next year we can be down a little or quite a bit. Remember that 6% is an average of both higher and lower annual growth.

Let's walk through an actual scenario—and the promised explanation of a sequence of returns risk. Imagine thinking this way about your 401k income back in 2000 when you hypothetically retired, and the market was doing fine. You based your financial planning on the above assumptions: the 401k will make 6% a year, and I'll use 5%. Then came the Tech Boom/Bust or the financial crisis of 2008. Pick your downturn period. In three consecutive years, the S&P 500 index dropped 9.10%, 11.89%, and 22.10%. (The S&P 500 Index is considered a reflection of the large-capitalization U.S. stock market.) If you don't adjust the amount of your withdrawals—if you keep withdrawing your 5%—the value of your portfolio is taking a hit from two directions simultaneously: you and the stock market. Enter the **sequence of returns risk**.

Assume you withdraw 5%, and your portfolio earns 5% or more each year. In that situation, you know you'll be in good shape. In fact, you may even be able to increase the dollar amount you are taking out each year. There is, however, a big difference between an *average* of 5% and the sequence in which we earn that 5%. What if over a 5-year period in retirement, you earned annual returns of -3%, -15%, +18%, +10%, and +15%? You still averaged 5%, but in your first two years of retirement, your portfolio dropped by 8% and 20% (the 5% withdrawals in addition to the 3% drop in the first year and 15% drop in the second year). Although your portfolio had three decent years of returns, fewer actual dollars were trying to earn that 18%, 15%, and 10%. To further compound that hole you want to dig out of, you're still withdrawing your 5%. Do you see the problem?

What I just described is the risk of the sequence of returns. You can't simply look at your average return and trust that you'll be OK in retirement. You can't count on the equity market to generate earnings according to your needs: it will throw different annual and even monthly returns at you. Your financial planner will help you fully understand this risk and then work with you to ensure that you don't wipe out your 401k due to the sequence of returns.

* * * * *

I hope you see the tremendous value of having an advisor who can have these conversations with you and help you navigate various possible scenarios. Once you develop a personal relationship with an advisor and he or she comes to know your individual goals and fears, you'll have these honest and therefore helpful discussions about your finances. Unless you're in the financial advising business, you need a trained and competent person you can trust to help you make good decisions and to speak the truth to you even when it isn't what you want to hear.

You also want your financial advisor to understand people. Almost everyone, for instance, has a hard time adjusting to change, and the concept of having a Paycheck Replacement Plan introduces change. One day you may need to adjust your lifestyle in order to sustain your retirement, but you don't need to make those adjustments now. If you start by keeping your initial retirement income the same as your working income, you won't be overwhelmed by the transition into retirement—and your transition to the next phase of retirement will be much easier.

CHAPTER 4

Longevity and Inflation

How Long Will You Live?

Your retirement planning would be much easier if you knew the exact day you would die. Then you'd know which pension option to select and when to start claiming Social Security. You'd figure out how much money you had left, divide it by the number of years of life you had left, and then live life to the fullest so you could die broke. You would have enjoyed every last penny you'd earned.

But, alas, you don't know when you'll die, and that's the challenge. You can use actuary tables and averages, but you're still gambling. So because you don't know how long you will live, you have to assume that you'll make it to 95 because you might! Some people with underlying health concerns may know they won't make it past 75, but if you're in good or even excellent health, you just may see 95 candles on your birthday cake, especially if your parents or aunt lived to be 100. That's why you have to make sure you won't be out of money if you live that long. As I've said, you don't want to run out of money before you run out of life. Your goal is to ensure that you don't become a burden to society or, more importantly, to your children and heirs.

Let's say you retire at 55 and live until you're 95. That's forty years—and you may not have even worked that many years! A police chief I knew about retired at age 55, and—the story goes—he seemed to be the wealthiest man in town because his public or government pension was so strong. But he hadn't saved while he was working. He didn't think he had to because he had a good pension. He ended up living until he was 95, and he wasn't the wealthiest man in town by a long shot.

Living on his pension would have worked out just fine if he had died younger. His pension did have an annual built-in cost-of-living adjustment, but his actual everyday expenses increased faster than his pension could keep up with. The police officer either didn't plan for the possibility of living that long, or he didn't know about the silent money killer: inflation (more on this later).

So we financial advisors do all our projections assuming that you'll live until 95. It's better to overestimate how long you'll live than underestimate it.

*   *   *   *   *

President Franklin Delano Roosevelt signed the Social Security Act in 1935, during the middle of the Great Depression. The program was designed as a social insurance program to pay retired workers aged 65 or older a continuing income in retirement. It was designed to help older workers who didn't have a pension move into retirement so that factories and businesses could hire younger workers and pay them lower wages. Interestingly, at that time, the retirement age was 65, but the average lifespan then was 58 for men and 62 for women.

Now, about 90 years later, these life expectancy numbers are different. Women are expected to live to 79 and men to 73. Because of this gradual increase in life expectancy, Social Security and the claiming options have changed. To be specific, we can take our Social Security benefit as early as age 62 or as late as age 70.

According to the Society of Actuaries, if a man is alive at 65, he can expect to live to age 83 (age 86 for women). However, if both a husband and wife are alive at 65, there's a 50% chance that at least one of you will make it to age 90 and an almost 25% chance that one of you will make it to age 95, with a very real possibility that you'll live into your late 90s. Clearly, these days we need to be sure your retirement plan will sustain one or both of you for 30+ years.

The Silent Killer

As I mentioned earlier, when you and your advisor do your planning, you have to plan for the silent killer of retirement plans: inflation. During certain periods, inflation was at the forefront of everyone's mind, but at other times inflation has still been present but much more silently.

During your working years, for instance, you probably didn't think much about inflation because a person's pay typically rises at the pace that inflation does. As you continued to get raises, you adjusted your spending and didn't notice inflation. Remember buying your first home and wondering how you'd manage those monthly payments? Fifteen years later, though, that same monthly mortgage expense is not as worrisome. Your income has increased, but that fixed cost stayed constant. A carton of milk or a gallon of gas, however, is *not* a fixed cost.

Let's look at how inflation has impacted the price of three everyday purchases:

Product	Average Price in 1995	Average Price in 2021	% Increase
Milk	$2.48	$3.55	43%
Postage Stamp	32 cents	55 cents	72%
Gas	$1.15 per gallon	$3.19 per gallon	177%

Based on the 26-year price difference shown in this chart, if you retired at 60 in 2021, a gallon of milk will cost $8.83 when you're 86. This difference of a few dollars plus the increased cost of several other inflated products will add up over the course of a year. If you don't plan for this and if your investments aren't keeping up with inflation, you'll deplete your retirement savings just by purchasing basic necessities. The value of your fixed-income money can't keep up with the inflated cost of living.

Inflation is defined as the long-term tendency of money to lose purchasing power. Retirees often suffer more than working people as inflation erodes the purchasing power of their fixed retirement income. Additionally, inflation can be consistent for several years and then suddenly shift up or down. The chart above shows the changes in inflation's impact from year to year. We easily lose track of how much inflation affects our income purchasing power. It truly is the silent killer. To illustrate, if we had an annual income of $50,000 and the annual inflation rate was 3%, inflation would diminish that spendable income over a 25-year period to $23,880.

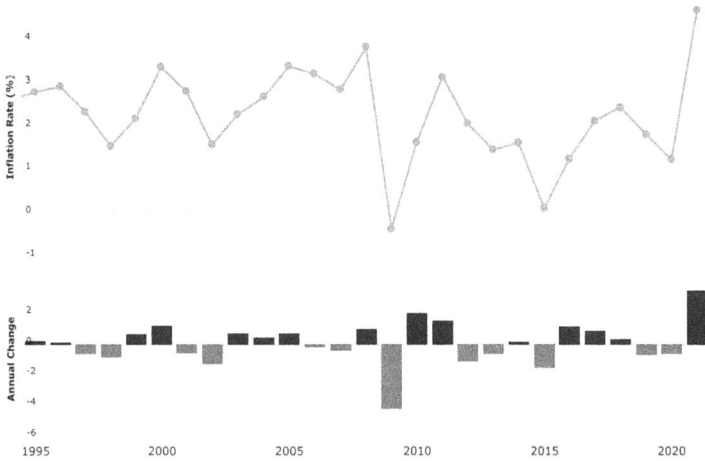

The Rule of 72 offers another way to consider the effects of inflation by helping us determine how long it takes for money's buying power to be cut in half. Let's say inflation is 4%. The Rule of 72 has us divide 72 by 4, which is it. So we see that it would take 18 years for a product to double in price. If you're retired for 35+ years, the cost of that product will double twice in that time. Say you have a car right now that you paid $50,000 for. When you're 18 years into retirement and need a new car, the price of a car might be $100,000. When you're 36 years into retirement, the price of that same car might be $200,000.

And remember: your Social Security and some pensions don't automatically adjust for inflation. Social Security is intended to adjust for inflation each year, but Congress must pass those cost-of-living adjustments for inflation, and years can go by without Congress acting on this matter. Depending on your employer, your pension may or may not adjust for inflation. Some pensions adjust for inflation based on the Consumer Price Index or a preset amount, but some pensions don't adjust at all.

Longevity & Inflation

Depending on the economic environment, some retirees can't afford to travel because the price of airline tickets is inflated. Other retirees who planned to travel bought an RV, but it sits in the driveway because the price of gas is too high. If you were still working, you might not be as worried about those inflated costs because your pay would have increased and would continue to. But what if you'd hoped to travel when you retired, but now your fixed income can't cover increased plane tickets and gas costs? You have to plan ahead so that dreams of traveling can actually happen. And planning ahead means making sure your investments are beating inflation. It's a race—and if inflation wins, you're out of money.

So let's demystify investing. I've met far too many people who sit on savings accounts because they're afraid of the market. I get it: the roller-coaster movement of the market scares people. Other folks have adopted their parents' mentality and are stuck there. If your parents lived through the Great Depression, they probably instilled in you the conviction that the stock market should not be trusted. But that was almost 100 years ago, and the world has changed. This Depression-era advice is outdated. You can't live well in today's world with a 1930s mentality. That old way of thinking doesn't match today's reality.

Furthermore, the significant drop in interest rates in recent years has created a bit of a crisis for people who have stayed out of equities or general stock market investing, who have kept money in savings account rather than investing in the market. Again, relying exclusively on savings accounts means that in the future years, you may not have enough to travel, help the kids, or afford all your retirement dreams.

Bottom line, sitting on your money for whatever reasons is not at all a playing-it-safe strategy. Sitting on your money only makes sense if you don't plan on living long or you're not wanting to leave assets to the kids. If you're relying only on savings accounts, inflation is going to beat you because you don't have any investments working for you.

* * * * *

Key to lower-stress investing (I'm not sure stress-free investing exists), understand that investing is about the big picture. Yes, you might see a loss on your quarterly or monthly statement now and then, but in the long run, you'll end up with a long-term bucket of money to pull from in retirement.

The challenge of living with equity investing comes with the constant overload of information. Watching the daily news, where the name of the game is to sell advertising, we can be paralyzed by fear and discouragement, paralyzed into inactivity and indecision. Have you noticed you hear more on the news when the market is correcting (going down) than you do about the market expanding (going up)?

When I began in the industry, I told my nurse clients who had invested in the stock market to put their unopened quarterly statements in a drawer and not open them until the end of the year. I knew they would be better off—they would be less stressed—if they looked at their long-term investments on an annual basis. Even better for all of us would be looking at the statements every three years. Either way, whether one year or three, we would be much better off than if we are watching the news channels and checking our investments daily.

Again, I gave this advice to the nurses 30 years ago when daily valuations weren't as available as they are today, but even they benefited from quarterly or annual glances at their savings. When those nurses opened their quarterly statements, they might react with "Uh-oh, that wasn't a good quarter." But the next quarterly statement might prompt, "Oh my! Look at all the money I made this quarter!"

If you choose to check your quarterly statements as they come out, you might respond out of fear and either lower the amount of your regular investments or change your investment behavior. With either of those moves, you lose money in the long run because you've pulled out money just as your investments might have been about to do well. Additionally, by slowing down your savings with one of those two actions, you aren't taking advantage of the benefits of dollar cost averaging (DCA).

What Is Dollar Cost Averaging?

Dollar-cost averaging (DCA) refers to what happens to a growing investment when a person invests the same amount of money during good times and bad. As a simple example of this consistent, systematic approach to investing, let's say you're investing $100 per month in an equity-based mutual fund. When you purchase your first index shares, the value is $2.50 per unit, and you purchase 40 units.

A month later, the value has dropped by 20% to $2.00 per unit. You receive your statement and see that you still have 40 units that are now valued at $2.00 a unit, for a grand total of $80. You invested $100, and you've lost $20. But step back and understand that you are not cashing out this money. In fact, you're still saving

$100, but now the units are on sale for $20 a unit. Guess what? You just added another 50 (not 40) units to your total.

So next month, when the market makes a huge rebound, those units—all 50 of them—are worth $3.00 a unit. Now you have 90 units worth $3.00 each for a total value of $270. Again, though, you are *not* selling yet. In fact, you're going to make another $100 investment that buys you 33 1/3 units, and now the value of a unit is $2.50 a unit, *exactly* where it was when you started. So with your standard $100, you purchase another 40 units, but now you look at your totals (also in the chart below). You have 163 1/3 units worth $2.50 a unit for a total value of $408.33, even though the unit value initially and today—$2.50 then and now—suggests that the index hasn't changed in four months. Granted, the $8.33 profit on your $400 investment is small, but imagine taking this consistent approach to investing for not just four months but for 30 years or longer. Focus on this big picture and the more distant horizon, and you won't be as worried about the day-to-day volatility of the market.

Investment/ Saving	Unit Value	# of Units Purchased	Total Units	Total Value
$100	$2.50	40		$100
$100	$2.00	50	90	$180
$100	$3.00	33	123	$370
$100	$2.50	40	163	$408.33

Let me add this about that big picture. According to Capital Research and Management Company, we know that, on average, the S&P 500 will have a 20% or more downturn about once every six years and a 15% downturn once every four years. Additionally, the equity market will have a 10% drop on average once a year.

Despite that pattern of downturns, from 1937 to June of 2021, the average return on the S&P 500 was 10.54%. But it only earned that return for the investors who did not move their investments or change their investment strategy.

Back in 1937, though, your parents or grandparents probably didn't worry about inflation the way you do now. Also, life expectancy wasn't what it is now. Living into your late 90s was rare, but today's healthcare increases our longevity. Based on those facts alone, you can't follow your parents' outdated ideas about investing because they probably weren't preparing to live to 98. They weren't preparing for 30+ years of retirement and the inflation that comes over that period of time. For instance, my grandfather retired in 1981 at age 65. He ended up having a heart attack and passing at age 67. He only had two years of "inflation" to worry about. Contrary, my father-in-law is an 87 year old former elementary school teacher. He recently told his family that he just hit the age where he has been retired as long as he actually worked. Now, however, we are retiring earlier and living longer. Dealing with inflation is a challenging reality.

Inflation isn't a concern if, like my grandfather, you only live a few years into retirement. But if you end up living until you're 95, inflation could be the silent killer of your lifestyle. Since inflation increases exponentially, your spending power will decrease more significantly the longer you live. That's why you need investments that will grow your money exponentially. Only then will you be able to withstand decades of inflation.

CHAPTER 5

Social Security

When Should You Take Social Security?

For many working adults, Social Security will provide a good portion of their final retirement income. In fact, for 1 in 4 older adults, Social Security currently makes up 90% of their retirement income. So decisions about Social Security need to be made very carefully. Your retirement and your spouse's well-being depend on it.

* * * * *

First, some background. President Franklin Roosevelt signed the Social Security Act into law on August 14, 1935, during the Great Depression. One of the many challenges of that era arose because we had young men graduating from college and looking for their first job (not many women were in the workforce in the '30s), but not many jobs were available.

At the same time, older men who were working in factories had not built up any retirement savings. If they stopped working, they'd have no income. They were literally working themselves to death. The only way for a young man to get a job was for someone to become too sick to work.

When Social Security was signed into law, the younger workers gladly paid some money out of their income to fund those people who needed to retire and, at the same time, create a fund that these now young workers would need 35 years later. Right away, though, older workers could use this social insurance as their replacement income to help fund their retirement.

Also—as I noted earlier—the plan was designed to provide income for people when they turned 65. However, in the '30s and '40s, life expectancy for a male was between 60 and 64 years of age. So some men—those who lived to 65—did receive Social Security, but many men did not.

* * * * *

Back to the present. When I sit down with clients, and we start talking about their retirement, I ask them when they plan to start taking their Social Security benefits. Most will say, "I guess when I'm 65." But why? The age of 65 is stuck in everyone's heads because that was the traditional start date for Social Security retirement income.

Remember, that number was chosen when most people didn't think about having other sources of income. For many decades, the retirement income consisted of Social Security, a company pension if you were lucky, and age of 65 was the norm. You just planned that on your 65th birthday, you'd get your gold watch from the company, carry your box of belongings out the office door, and receive your first Social Security check.

But remember, you have to qualify for Social Security. You do that by earning 40 credits during your working years when you are paying an indexed minimum level of Social Security taxes. You earn one credit every quarter of the year that you work or four credits a year. In 2022, you would have earned 1 credit if you made at least $1,510 in a given quarter. Both you and your employer paid 6.2% of your salary (for a total of 12.4%) into the Social Security fund. This minimum income requirement will change each year based on adjustments for inflation.

Once you have your 40 credits—your 10 years of work—you qualify for Social Security. The monthly benefit calculation will be based on several factors, including the number of years you worked, average indexed earnings over those years, and your age when you start claiming your benefit.

You can start taking Social Security Benefits as early as age 62, but that permanent amount will be less than the full benefits that you become entitled to receive when you reach your full retirement age (FRA). Your full retirement age is between 65 and 67 depending on your birth year. And I'll explain.

Working in Retirement

In 1983, as part of the Social Security Reform bill, Social Security raised the full retirement age—and therefore the ability to collect full Social Security retirement benefits—from age 65 to 67, depending on your date of birth. If you were born after 1960, your age of full benefit was moved from age 65 to age 67.

If your date of birth was before 1960, your full retirement age is somewhere between 65 and 67. Even with this change, many people use the age of 65 as the retirement age when they do their financial planning.

Under this 1983 legislation, once you started your Social Security benefit and then decided to work in retirement, an earned income test was required. If you made over a certain amount of money, your Social Security benefit was reduced or eliminated. Because of this restriction, many people didn't work once they retired.

In 2000, Congress passed the Senior Citizens Freedom to Work Act, allowing workers to claim Social Security benefits at their full retirement age (whatever age that may be) but continue to work and earn an income.

* * * * *

Most people know they can take Social Security as early as age 62, yet few people consider the benefits of waiting. Depending on your health and how much longer you'd like to work, it may make sense to postpone your benefit for a couple of years.

Let's consider the worker with a birthdate after 1960 and an FRA of 67. Taking Social Security before age 67 will mean a reduction in those benefits of about 4.5% to 5% per year for each year prior to the full retirement age. If this worker begins taking Social Security at age 62, her benefit will be reduced by 5% per year x 5 years (67 FRA - 62 = 5), or 25%. In other words, her Social Security benefit at age 62 would be 75% of what her full retirement benefit would have been at 67. The advantage is she will have income sooner rather than later. However, her cost-of-living adjustments will be based on that lower benefit amount *for the rest of her life*. In addition, she may face a possible reduction of her Social Security benefit OR if her earned income in retirement exceeds her indexed limit, addressed in the next section.

The bottom line is that taking Social Security at 62 and getting that income stream started early may look like a smart move, but if you end up living for a long time, you will have missed out on a lot of money over those years. Most people should, if possible, wait as long as they can before taking Social Security. You may not have the choice, but if you do, if you are able to wait, the benefits will be greater.

* * * * *

Let's revisit the Social Security Income Earnings Test as well as another challenge that comes with taking Social Security before your full retirement age. The amount of income you are allowed to earn before you begin to lose some of your Social Security benefit is indexed each year. If you earn too much based on that index, you could end up losing all your Social Security benefit for that given year. For every $2 you earn above that indexed income limit, your Social Security benefit is reduced by $1. Yes, that's a 50% cut in your Social Security benefit! So if you're inclined to work after you retire, carefully consider the long-term impact of that potential cut. Let me give you an example of the income earnings test and how the penalty is imposed.

When you retire at 64, you start taking your Social Security benefit, but then you decide to go back to work. For the sake of this example, I'll say that your Social Security benefit is $2,000 a month, which comes to $24,000 a year. You earn $30,000 a year at your new job, but the earnings limit for Social Security—to keep the math simple—is $20,000. (For the tax year 2023, a retiree's income limit is $21,240.) Since you earned $10,000 above the limit, your Social Security benefit is reduced by $5,000. But instead of giving you a lower amount each month, Social Security continues to pay you $2,000 per month beginning in January until you hit $19,000 total for the year ($24,000 Social Security benefit - $5,000 reduction because you earned $10,000 above the limit).

How exactly does this play out, though? Let's say you filed your 2020 income taxes by April 15, 2021. Only then did the Social Security Administration know your actual earned income for 2020, so you would pay the penalty for exceeding the indexed income limit in 2022. The count toward your $19,000 limit began in January 2022. You received $2000 a month from January through September (a total of $18,000), $1000 in October, and then nothing in November and December. In April 2022, however, you completed your income tax returns for 2021. The Social Security Administration then learned your total income for 2021 and applied the same indexed income limit test for that year's earnings.

In 2022—when you received no Social Security income during November and December—you may have struggled a bit to put a turkey on the table and buy presents, especially if you stopped working in the early part of 2022. But if you stopped working in October 2022, you'd be hit especially hard with an indexed income limit penalty because the Social Security reduction for 2023 will be based on your ten-month income in 2022. You can't rely on your Social Security check in this situation.

Various adjustments could be applied, but you can avoid all this if you wait until you reach your FRA to start collecting Social Security. Once you reach your FRA, you can earn unlimited income without it having any negative effect on your Social Security benefit.

* * * * *

Again, I usually advise my clients to wait to turn on Social Security even if they decide to retire early. Why? They need to make sure this retirement gig sticks! If you get bored after a year or two and decide to head back to work, there's a chance you'll lose some of your benefits. If you're going to earn less than the limit, maybe from a part-time job, you don't have to worry. But if you haven't quite hit the FRA, we don't want to turn Social Security on until you're entirely sure you won't ever go back to work at a job where you will earn above the limit.

Worth noting, however, is the fact that as of this writing, you get one do-over with Social Security. If you start receiving your Social Security benefit and change your mind, you can pay that money back within 12 months and act like it never happened. Your Social Security will continue to accrue age credits, and the eventual benefit will continue to grow.

Why Take Social Security Early?

Although I usually advise my clients to wait to turn on Social Security, in some situations it does make sense to turn on Social Security early. If you're not in good health and want to preserve your retirement assets for your heirs, turning on Social Security sooner rather than later might be the right decision for you. Since

Social Security has no death benefit and the state of your health suggests you're not going to live to 95, it may be smarter for you to live off Social Security and save your assets for your heirs. You may also need to turn on Social Security early if you haven't saved enough for retirement. Clearly, your specific situation is the boss. You need to put food on your table, so you may have no choice but to take Social Security early.

Another reason people take Social Security early, though, is FOMO, the fear of missing out. People are afraid that Social Security won't be there for them when they need it, so they want to get whatever amount of their money they can as soon as possible. But Social Security is not going away. Payments might be reduced, but it's not going away. So don't decide to take Social Security early because you're afraid the program will end. The disappearance of Social Security is not a realistic scenario.

That said, we do need Congress and the president to make some tough decisions just as our leaders did with the 1983 reform. Ideas worth considering are adjusting the claiming age for the younger work force, increasing the Social Security tax for both employees and employers, tying some of the growth to the equity market, and increasing or eliminating the income tax cap.

Clearly, some reasons for taking Social Security early are more valid than others. Still, the decision is yours.

Why Delay Social Security?

Now let me talk about some good reasons for waiting to claim your Social Security benefit. To begin, understand that your Social Security statement will specify your benefit at three ages:

62 (or your current age if you are older), your FRA, and 70. Each year you delay *after* your FRA is a ***forever*** increase in your benefit of between 4% and 5% per year. That increase, along with cost-of-living adjustments, makes the option to delay Social Security more attractive.

As you consider this option, be sure to know your break-even age. This break-even point is the age when your cumulative benefits from claiming Social Security at 67 or later surpass the benefits you'd get from taking the smaller retirement benefit five years earlier when you were 62. For instance, let's compare the typical 2.7% annual average compounded increase on a monthly $2100 Social Security benefit at age 62 to the same 2.7% annual average compounded increase on a $3800 monthly benefit at age 70. If you receive a 2.7% increase on $2100, that would be an annual adjustment of a monthly increase of $56.70. That same 2.7% increase of $3800 is almost twice that amount: $102.60 per month. (Cost of living raises will be added to that amount and compounded as well, further increasing your benefit at age 70 and after.) You can see how quickly the *total* accumulated amount received by the worker who first claimed at 70 would catch up to the total accumulated amount received by the worker claiming at age 62. Depending on the amount of your monthly benefit, your break-even age will be anywhere between 78 and 82 years old. So if you believe you'll live to somewhere within that window of 78 years through 82 years, your net gain will be more if you wait until 70 to take Social Security. If you don't live to 78, you would have been better off taking Social Security at some point before you turned 70. Clearly, the state of your health plays a part in this decision.

Again, we don't know when you'll die, so the decision you make is a bit of a gamble. But if you have health issues and don't expect to live until 78, it may be wise to consider taking Social Security earlier. If you're married and you expect at least one of you to survive until 78 or 82, it makes sense to have at least one spouse wait until 70 to turn on Social Security because the surviving spouse will receive the higher Social Security benefit of the two. This is the Barbell Approach, which I'll discuss in the next section of this chapter.

When I'm advising clients, I encourage them to start taking Social Security no later than age 70. If they—if you—don't need the money now, it's better to take larger payments later in retirement when income might be less and expenses, especially healthcare expenses, might be more.

* * * * *

If you're thinking about delaying Social Security payments, another consideration is the required minimum distribution (RMD) and the forced income it generates. Depending on your birth year and due to the recent changes of the Secure Act 1.0 and Secure Act 2.0, your RMD will begin sometime between the ages of 70 ½ and 75. When you reach RMD age, you must begin to take these RMDs. Every retirement plan account owner must withdraw these minimum amounts annually regardless of income need or asset level.

One strategy involves delaying the start of Social Security, letting those built in deferral benefits grow and instead pulling money out of qualified retirement accounts *before* your RMDs need to be withdrawn. Doing so will reduce the amount of the eventual

RMDs you'll have to take. A forced distribution on the resulting smaller amount would reduce your eventual forced taxable income. That taxable income is a factor when you turn on Social Security at age 70 because that benefit has increased each year of your delay (due to your increased age and cost-of-living adjustments), and you'll find yourself with a much more tax-efficient income if you've been withdrawing from your qualified retirement accounts before you were forced to.

You'll find a more thorough discussion of RMDs in chapter 8.

* * * * *

I have one last consideration for people who have a large debt (say, a mortgage) and are choosing to work late into retirement. If you find yourself working past your FRA and even though you are continuing to work, you may want to turn on that extra Social Security income and have *all* that extra income go directly toward paying off that outstanding debt.

Many people choose to work further into retirement because of a huge debt that is causing them to lose sleep. These folks are extra motivated to have that debt paid off before they retire. Paying off an outstanding debt may be a better use of this extra Social Security income than getting the benefit of delaying Social Security income even with the higher cost-of-living adjustment and the long-term income benefit that comes with the delay.

The Barbell Approach

A key factor in planning for retirement is the survivor benefit that Social Security offers. When a spouse passes away, the surviving spouse is able to keep the higher of the two Social Security benefits. When you complete a financial plan, you will definitely want to map out what happens if the spouse with the lower benefit takes Social Security early and the spouse with the higher benefit starts Social Security at age 70. This is the Barbell Approach: the spouses claim their benefits at opposite ends of the age spectrum, specifically age 62 and age 70.

I'll share an example from my own life. My wife stopped working as a nurse when she had our first child, so she does qualify for Social Security. But since she only has about 10 working years of credit, her Social Security benefit will be low. I've been working since I was 16, and I will most likely work into my early 70s, so I'll receive a very high Social Security benefit. We plan to take my wife's benefit when she turns 62 and enjoy having some extra spending money while I'm still working. Since my wife isn't working, she doesn't have to worry about the earnings test. My full retirement age is 67, but I'm going to wait until I'm 70 to take it. If I happen to pass away between 62 and 70, my wife will still get my higher benefit. Technically, she will receive her benefit and an extra payment that is the difference between her benefit and what I was receiving or was going to receive.

If both spouses are healthy, you could both wait to take Social Security until age 70. But if you want the surviving spouse to get the higher amount, why would you both wait until 70? Enjoy the lower-benefit spouse's money in the meantime and rest assured knowing that the higher benefit will be coming and will continue no matter how long either of you lives.

Coordinating Social Security & Pensions

Social Security is a different issue if you have a government pension. Teachers, police officers, firefighters, city employees, and other government employees are not allowed to receive both their pension *and* Social Security payments. Depending on your employer, you may or may not have paid into Social Security. You may have just paid into your pension, so you won't get Social Security in addition to that. Note: Some employers have paid in to *both* Social Security *and* the public pension. Many federal employees, for instance, have paid into FERS (Federal Employee Retirement System) *and* Social Security. Those individuals will have special planning needs and advantages.

If you are receiving a pension and are married to someone who receives Social Security, you will have to carefully decide if you want to receive your pension based on just *your* life or if you want some type of survivor benefit for your spouse. *If the spouse with the pension dies first, the surviving spouse's Social Security could be affected because he/she will now get part of the pension, and a person can't be receiving both.*

It is also crucial to discuss with a financial advisor the Windfall Elimination Provision (WEP) and the Government Offset Provision (GOP). As you'll see in chapter 7 when I unpack both of these rules, every married person who is receiving a government pension needs to consider the long-term benefit and ramifications of their choices in order to avoid a potential loss of income.

Divorce and Death Benefits

If you were married for at least 10 years and you're now divorced and not remarried, you're entitled to your ex-spouse's Social Security benefit, and that person never even has to know that you claimed it. Your claim does not affect your ex-spouse's benefit or his/her new spouse's benefit.

For example, Johnny Carson was married four times. Three of those marriages lasted 10 years, and the fourth lasted 9 ½. If they didn't remarry, each of those three wives could have claimed Johnny Carson's Social Security benefit at whatever age they chose and without Johnny or the other ex-spouses ever knowing. And that benefit would not have been divided among them: each woman would have received the full Social Security benefit. Yes, the government is on the hook for three times what Johnny paid in, and even if all three ex-wives claimed the benefit, their claims would not have affected Johnny's benefit whenever he applied.

In addition to addressing divorced couples, Social Security provides benefits for widows/widowers and other surviving family members after a person passes. These benefits vary depending on the circumstances of the beneficiaries and the age of the deceased. I know that from experience. I was still in high school when my father passed. In those first few years after his death, some of his Social Security benefits helped my mother, my two brothers, and me.

* * * * *

The main take-away from this chapter is the basic fact that turning on Social Security is a complicated decision. In fact, Social Security is like a puzzle—and it's a different puzzle for every person. In addition to each retiree's situation being unique, every decision has pros and cons.

There is no one-size-fits-all answer. What's best for someone else may not be at all good for you. And you can't make decisions that will impact the rest of your life based on something you heard on the news or on what your neighbor recommends.

Again, everyone's situation is different; everyone's circumstances are unique. It's the job of a financial advisor to help you understand the trade-offs of various options and to enable you to make educated and wise decisions so that you will enjoy the best-case-scenario retirement.

Note: If you are working with a financial advisor, ask for a personalized Social Security analysis. Then the three of you together (the advisor, you, and your spouse) can figure out the best time for the two of you to take Social Security based on your income needs, your current assets, and your ages. Avoid any knee-jerk reaction to turning 65. Instead, look at the various options; lay out all the pros and cons before you decide. Only after walking through all the possibilities will you be able to make an informed decision.

CHAPTER 6

Healthcare in Retirement

Medicare

One of the biggest concerns for people entering retirement is healthcare: how will they afford it? For people who are retired, Medicare starts at age 65. If you're still working at 65, you probably still have health insurance from your company, and you'll continue to use that healthcare coverage until you do retire.

Even if you're still working, you must contact the Social Security Administration during the 6-month window—three months before and three months after your 65th birthday—to let them know that you should be in the Medicare queue. If you fail to contact them, you will incur a *permanent penalty* on your Medicare premiums. Most of the time, Medicare will contact you, but be aware of that 6-month window so you don't miss it and end up paying a penalty the rest of your life. If Medicare contacts you—or you contact them—let Medicare know that you're still working and don't yet need the coverage.

Original Medicare includes Part A and Part B, but other parts have since been added:

- Part A is hospital insurance that covers inpatient hospital care, some skilled nursing facility care, hospice care, and home healthcare. Except for a deductible that will be due for each hospital stay, Part A comes at no cost for most retirees.

- Part B is the medical insurance provided for a monthly fee that's typically deducted from your Social Security payment. If you have yet to start receiving your Social Security benefit, you'll be billed for your Medicare coverage. Part B covers part of your doctor appointments, outpatient care, lab services, home healthcare, durable medical equipment, and preventative services.

- Part D is drug coverage. It's not included with original Medicare, so you have to either purchase a drug plan in addition to original Medicare or choose a Medicare Advantage Plan that includes drug coverage.

- A Medicare Advantage Plan (Part C) is an approved plan provided by a private company. These Medicare Advantage plans include Part A, Part B, and sometimes Part D. Some plans also include vision and dental services.

- Medicare Supplemental Insurance is extra insurance that you can buy from a private company to help cover your remaining out-of-pocket costs.

If you've carefully planned for retirement and done a great job saving money, I hope you're thinking, "We aren't skimping on health insurance. We're getting the Cadillac!" You're entering the phase of life where you might need healthcare more than you've ever needed it before, and you definitely don't want to run into any problems because you went for a cheaper option.

The Medicare Earnings Test

You need to be aware of and plan for the Medicare Earnings Test. If your income—your combined working income, pension income, required minimum distribution income, and/or investment income—is above the Medicare limit, you'll have to pay a surcharge tax on your Medicare benefit. A financial advisor can help you control that income flow so it stays under the threshold.

As I discussed in the previous chapter and will discuss in greater detail in chapter 8, one possible option for controlling income flow is taking money out of your IRAs *before* your RMDs begin. Doing so may help you avoid boosting your income over the Medicare earnings threshold when you are forced to start those taxable withdrawals.

For higher-income earners, that Medicare surcharge increases at different income thresholds. The result can be extra monthly charges per person of anywhere from $68 to $400 per month for your Medicare. Some people may not be concerned about paying this surcharge, but I believe we should minimize any and all extra charges if possible. If you're making so much money—either while you're still working or during retirement—that you're way above the Medicare threshold, you may not be concerned about the surcharge because you can easily afford it. But if you're only a little bit over the threshold or near the next level, try as much as possible to avoid that surcharge.

* * * * *

Understandably, healthcare costs are the #1 worry for early retirees. If you retire before 65, you'll still have a few years before you qualify for Medicare. In that case, you'll need private health insurance to cover your healthcare costs until you turn 65. That health insurance might cost as much as $1200 a month, which is very different from Medicare at $144 a month.

So if you're retiring before age 65, you definitely need to factor health insurance costs into your plan. Many couples may have one spouse retire early while the other remains employed simply to have employer-sponsored health insurance for both of them. This approach could save them thousands of dollars.

If you want to retire before 65, but the cost of healthcare is preventing you, working part-time might be an option. I encourage my clients to look into the possibility of working 20 hours a week and maintaining their employer-paid health insurance.

The Importance of Maintaining Your Health

It would be irresponsible to talk about health insurance costs without cautioning you to take good care of yourself. Your health affects your lifestyle as well as your healthcare costs, specifically the amount of money you'll be paying for your drugs, hospital or doctor visits, and co-pays.

So how healthy is your lifestyle? Be sure you're exercising and staying up to date with annual checkups because taking care of your health will reduce the cost of healthcare in retirement. That said, some health issues are completely out of your control, but you don't want to blow your savings on healthcare costs for issues that could have been prevented.

Also, if you have big retirement plans like traveling or taking up a new activity (pickle ball, anyone?), you want to be sure you're healthy enough to do whatever you want to do. I know too many people who had many wonderful retirement plans that didn't work out because they didn't take care of themselves. Work on maintaining a healthy lifestyle so you can enjoy a rich and full retirement.

The Danger of Healthcare Cost Inflation

The cost of healthcare will increase over the course of your retirement years, and healthcare costs increase at a level faster than inflation. If the inflation rate is 3% per year, we assume in our projections that healthcare costs are increasing between 5% and 7% per year.

From 1935 to 2022, medical care saw an average inflation rate of 4.67% per year. Medical care that cost $1,000 in 1935 would cost $21,614 in 1995… and $53,123 in 2022. Clearly, the reality of medical inflation has to be factored into your retirement plan.

Paying for Long-Term Care

Most people don't want to think about long-term care, but we absolutely must consider it.

First, some background about you. Are your parents still alive? How long did they live? Are they in a long-term care facility? Did/

do they live at home with you? In light of your answers, consider what your situation might look like when you're their age.

How long do you think you'll live? With improvements in medical care, chances are good that you will be living many years longer than your parents. So will you need long-term care? The Department of Health and Human Services (HHS) projects that one in three people will require long-term care. You can't ignore this possibility, and you can't count on Medicare to cover that cost.

So what exactly is long-term care? Long-term care—either in your home or in a nursing home—provides needed help with any of these six assisted daily living (ADL) activities:

- Eating
- Bathing
- Transferring
- Dressing
- Toileting
- Continence

Insurance is available to help cover the cost of long-term care. Many people wrongly believe, though, that long-term care insurance only covers care in a nursing home. Most people want to stay in their home and have help come in, and—some good news here—most insurance policies cover in-home help.

The cost of long-term care varies based on the type of care you need and where you live. I have a client in Southern California who pays $14,000 a month for care (that's almost $170,000 a year) because she has dementia. She needs her own room and a nurse readily available at all times. That kind of care is expensive—and it's the kind of care that you or your spouse might need someday. Most of us don't want this financial burden to fall on our children.

* * * * *

As you look ahead, realize that one of three things is going to happen:

1. You will need long-term care.
2. You will die.
3. You will not need long-term care, you will live a long time, and you may run out of money.

Again—and contrary to what you might think—long-term care is not covered by Medicare.

Many states have Medicaid, but those programs vary by state. If your state does have some type of Medicaid that helps with long-term care, that help will be limited. Also, Medicaid won't even consider helping unless you have exhausted much of your assets. Also, with Medicaid you won't be able to choose the facility and therefore the quality of the care you receive. You definitely don't want that decision made for you! You've worked too hard for too long to spend your last years in a subpar situation with subpar care. You need to think about long-term care insurance.

* * * * *

Two types of long-term care insurance are on the market: traditional and hybrid.

Traditional pay-as-you-go long-term care is like car insurance: you kind of hope you get into an accident so the money doesn't go to waste. If you don't end up needing the care—if you don't have a long-term care event—you spent all that money on insurance that you didn't use. That money is gone. Clearly, traditional long-term care insurance has its limitations.

Insurance companies started creating these products in the '80s when long-term care needs became more prevalent. The problem was, these companies priced their products so people could and would buy them. The companies, however, really didn't know how much money they were going to need to fully cover all the claims that might come their way. These companies simply gave consumers what they were asking for. Then, when nursing homes were starting to be built in the '60s, those facilities turned out to be quite expensive for the average person. People approaching retirement—the insurance companies' target market—needed insurance to pay for this huge expense.

Fast-forward to the point when claims on all those policies started being made. In many cases, companies had to cancel the insurance policy, increase the premiums, or make the claims process cumbersome. This may be the reason so many people are disenchanted with long-term care insurance. They've heard horror stories about their parents or someone they know who tried to make claims, jumped through lots of hoops, but never received any financial help—or who paid a ton for the insurance and then never needed the coverage.

Many insurance companies these days offer long-term care policies that are quite inexpensive if you buy them when you're between the ages of 55 and 60. These long-term policies are purchased with regular annual or monthly premiums, and, typically, these are group policies. Read the fine print because as you get older, the company may raise the prices and make the cost difficult, if not impossible, to afford—perhaps at the very time you need it most. The company may ask you to increase your premium for the same coverage, or it may reduce the coverage but keep the same cost. Be sure to read the fine print.

Many clients have come to us with these pay-as-you-go long-term care policies and asked what they should do. They're facing a hard decision based only on an educated guess of how long they will live. Another factor is the reality that they may have already poured a lot of money into this policy.

* * * * *

If you're fortunate and don't experience a long-term care event, you're going to wish you could get back at least part of the money you put into long-term care insurance. An option to consider—an option that covers all three end-of-life scenarios we looked at—is a hybrid policy.

A hybrid policy is a long-term care insurance policy with a small life insurance component. You will pay into the policy for a certain period, for 3, 5, 10, or 20 years. Once that selected period ends, you're done paying. You can also set up the plan by making a one-time deposit. A hybrid policy is not like a traditional policy where you pay for it until you die or until you have a long-term care event.

A hybrid plan also includes cost-of-living adjustments (COLAs) that can automatically increase the benefit by 3% to 5% per year.

These COLAs are necessary because you need less coverage today than you'll need when you're 85.

If you're shopping around, you want to be sure the hybrid policy you choose will ultimately provide you with a bucket of money. If you can create a bucket of $180,000 that's going to be paid out over six years, that's $30,000 a year. What if you don't need $30,000? What if you only need $15,000 because you only need part-time care to come into your home? That bucket of money can last a little longer than you initially thought. And if you pass before ever needing the coverage, your spouse or heirs will receive a small insurance policy. At least then some of your payments return to your family in the form of tax-free insurance. This long-term care policy with a life insurance rider may serve you well however the end of your life plays out.

Another benefit of some hybrid policies kicks in when you've held the policy for at least 5 years. Many times you can get back at least some of the money you've paid into it whenever you want. If you need money and no longer want or feel you'll need the long-term care policy, you can get that money back. Also, many policies offer a spousal discount. You can also find a joint long-term care policy with your spouse that creates a bucket of money that either one of you can pull from.

In summary, healthcare concerns and the decisions you make are fundamental to your retirement planning—and one of the biggest risks you'll consider. Be aware of the risks and be educated about options and solutions as you discuss retirement with your spouse and advisor.

CHAPTER 7

If You Have a Pension

Fewer people today have an employer pension than folks in our parents' and grandparents' generations did. If you are among those who do have the benefit of a pension, it's critical that you understand your options, the different payout choices, and how it will impact your overall retirement income plan.

Two different types of pension plans exist: public and private. Public pension plans are available for different types of government employees. The private pension plans that are still available are for nonpublic employers at both for-profit and nonprofit organizations.

Public Pensions

In agencies at every level of government—federal, state, and local—employees often have a public pension. The most common pensions for people working in California are CalPERS and CalSTRS. Certain counties may have their own pension plans. For instance, LA County employees have LACERA, and Orange County employees have OCERA.

Public pensions often include a cost-of-living adjustment: the pension income will increase over time to offset inflation.

The disadvantage of a public pension is that you have to depend on that particular governmental entity—and the prowess of its investment committee—for the management of the investment program that's providing the pension. For CalSTRS and CalPERS, that entity is the State of California. If the market's down, your benefit might be reduced because it depends on the underlying investments of the fund and the assumptions about growth that the State's investment committee made. (In contrast, Social Security is based on the claims-paying ability of the US government.)

For the most part, if you're getting a public pension, you will probably receive very little or no Social Security benefit. Some governmental entities pay into both Social Security and your public pension. In those situations, you will receive both, but the pension may mean a reduction in your Social Security payment. In general, people receive one source of income or the other.

The Windfall Elimination

If you're married to someone who may receive Social Security, you'll have to think carefully about what type of pension benefit to claim when you retire. If you take a joint pension on your public pension because you don't want to leave your spouse with less income when you pass, your spouse's Social Security could take a hit at that point.

In other words, if you're a public employee, you will receive the full CalPERS/CalSTRS benefit while you're alive, and your spouse will get his/her full Social Security benefit. But when you pass and your spouse continues to receive your public pension, your spouse's Social Security could get hit by the government offset provision, which is the spousal equivalent of the Windfall Elimination (see next paragraph). The government is trying to prevent people from taking from both the public pension and Social Security if they did not pay into both at the same time.

Let me explain the **Windfall Elimination**. Let's assume you have 20 years in public service and 20 years in private service. You will have credit in both your pension and Social Security, and you can claim benefits from both governmental agencies. You'll have to see what your total public pension benefit is before you can figure out whether your Social Security will be reduced. The government sets a limit on the total amount of Social Security you'll be able to collect. Sometimes you will not see this actual offset until you have chosen your public pension benefit. This is because you typically claim your pension benefit a couple years before age 62 and before you talk to the Social Security office.

I've seen firefighters blindsided by this unfortunate surprise way too often. If you're a firefighter, for instance, you might have joined the fire academy at 30 and retired at 60. Before the academy, though, you logged your 10 years of working in the private sector and paying into Social Security. Now you also have 30 years of CalPERS benefits from working as a firefighter, and that pension may mean receiving 90% of your final firefighter income. Applying the Windfall Elimination to this situation reduces the Social Security benefit significantly, if not eliminating it altogether.

One more point about Social Security. As we begin to plan our retirement income, we need to remember that Social Security is indexed to the current day's dollars. So although your income was lower in your younger working years and the Social Security benefit was based on that number, the income does index up. You still have those early Social Security credits, but it is based on an indexed income. So when people compare their Social Security income against the projected pension, most of them are OK with losing the Social Security money. In the example above, the firefighter most likely will *not* receive any Social Security benefit.

* * * * *

Now let's look at how the **government offset provision** (GPO) can affect the spousal income when the government employee who has a pension passes. Let's say a husband and wife are a firefighter and a nurse, respectively. The firefighter has a joint CalPERS public pension. The nurse has 40 years of Social Security from working at the hospital. She has the highest possible Social Security benefit she can receive because her income constantly increased and because she paid into Social Security at the annual limit each year. This consistent maximum Social Security contribution from both her paycheck and her employer's contribution will mean a very high Social Security benefit at her FRA age.

When the firefighter passes away, his wife will get the joint benefit from his pension. This is good. However, alternatively, if the wife with Social Security passes, the husband's survivor benefit from Social Security would most likely be reduced because of his public pension. This is where the GPO comes into play.

During the retirement planning process, a financial advisor can help a couple determine how the first spouse's passing will affect the survivor's income and what changes may have to be made at that point. Again, the joint pension *may* have been the right choice, but this couple would have been wise to proactively run the numbers, play out some unfortunate what-if scenarios, and see how the survivor's income and assets would be affected in each case.

Pension Maximization

So what can the firefighter do to ensure that his widow doesn't lose some of her Social Security benefits when he claims his pension? This couple could use a strategy called **pension maximization**. Married couples use this option if one spouse receives a pension and one spouse receives a larger Social Security benefit.

To take advantage of this strategy, the firefighter in our example will choose to take 100% of the pension benefit on his life as a *single* life instead of opting for the joint life option. He will then take the difference between his 100% and the benefit he would have received in the joint plan and use that money to buy a life insurance policy. His wife can still receive her full Social Security benefit. When the firefighter dies, his wife keeps her full Social Security benefit, but she also receives her husband's life insurance money **tax-free**. It may make more senses in this situation to have the life insurance on the Social Security spouse. As we discussed above, then when the Social Security spouse passes, the survivor with a public pension will most likely have their survivor Social Security benefit reduced. Obviously, you will want to look at the numbers as every situation will be different.

Each double-income retirement situation needs to be analyzed to see if the difference between the pension benefit and the amount of a life insurance benefit warrants the single-life decision about the pension instead of the joint plan. Obviously, much of this depends on the retiring pensioner's age and health as well as how the spouse invests the insurance benefits when the pensioner passes. Again, the advice of a financial planner who can run the models may make a lot of sense for a married couple.

Private Pensions

Private pensions don't give rise to the same challenge of balancing pension benefits and Social Security benefits that public pensions do. Since your private pension doesn't come from the government, you're not taking twice from the government when you receive both your pension and your Social Security benefit.

As stated above, private pensions are less common these days than in the past. Twenty and thirty years ago, pensions were more prevalent. Unions and corporations worked together to make sure their employees had a path to eventual retirement. Retirees would rely on pensions and Social Security to replace about 60% to 70% of their income. The idea was, you would retire, and the company would still pay your wages.

But these private companies assumed a great deal of liability with these pensions. They had to invest their assets wisely enough to be able to cover their promise of that eventual benefit. (The State of California's investment committee has the same task for CalPERS and CalSTRS.) The amount of the private company's monthly pension would be based on the retiree's age, years employed, and the factor—written into the particular pension plan—used to calculate the benefit. Actuarily, in order to provide every employee with a lifetime income after 65, the company had to make a best-guess as to the interest rate they'd be working with. When the market didn't cooperate with that assumption and the pensions didn't grow as anticipated, these pensions became underfunded.

Because of this risk and the liability of funding a retirement for the lifetime of their retired employees, many companies are freezing their private pensions—or already have. A frozen pension plan guarantees the benefits you earned during your working years but does not give you credit for your service after the pension plan is frozen. I'll give you an example.

Let's say you start working for a company at age 25 and then, when you're 45, they freeze your pension. When you retire at age 65, you still get the 20 years of pension credit you earned from age 25 to 45, but you receive no credit for the years you served beyond those 20 years. (It's worth noting that some companies have eliminated pensions altogether by totally cashing them out.)

By freezing or eliminating pensions, companies transfer the risk of funding retirement to employees. The risk of managing underlying investments is transferred to the employees via the 401k where the liability and challenges of investing that money are on you, the owner of your own 401k. Your company is depositing money in an account, but it's up to you to choose what to do with it and how to invest it. Rather than your employer, you yourself are responsible for making sure that money lasts the rest of your life. A cautionary tale would be to *not* put all of your retirement investment money into the money market and stable value funds. Using a balanced, diversified approach of investment vehicles, similar to what pension managers do, could be an appropriate alternative for these employer-provided funds.

In this author's opinion, most of the time these days companies are not making sure their employees are well educated about how to invest for retirement. Many companies have completely washed their hands of the responsibility. Too many times employees are left without the tools they need to decide how to take care of their family for the rest of their life. Both the lack of information and the absence of this skill set add to the stress as employees consider the end of their working career.

That said, I am seeing more and more companies recognizing the challenge their employees face, and these companies have begun to provide financial wellness tools either online or onsite with a hired firm. I applaud firms that are recognizing the serious need and acting on it, and it's been a privilege to be involved in some of those efforts. Despite this progress, we still see many company decision-makers using a price-per-pound approach to their retirement plans and the education their employees need. In other words, more concerned about the lowest price of the 401k services, these companies strip down benefits that might have helped their employees' overall financial health of their employees. Those organizations leave their employees to fend for themselves as they're making very important retirement investment decisions. I believe those organizations need to provide their employees with greater educational support and more opportunities to work with retirement planning professionals.

One additional point. If you have a pension, that's a big advantage when it comes to retirement planning. A significant disadvantage of a private pension, however, is the absence of a cost-of-living adjustment. In fact, I don't know if I've ever seen a private pension that includes a cost-of-living adjustment. Usually, the benefit a person chooses at the start of retirement is what that person will be getting at age 90 or until he/she passes.

Also, as we discussed previously, during a person's 25 or 35 years of retirement, inflation is a factor we need to plan for. If a private pension is your primary source of income, you'll need to plan for the gap between that static pension income and the cost-of-living increases that you will see over time. Finally, with private pensions, many times you won't have a death benefit either.

Private pensions offer much more limited payment options than public ones do. About half the time, you'll have the option of a lump-sum payout, and half the time your only option will be a lifetime income. You'll usually have to decide lump-sum or lifetime and single or joint pension within 90 days of your retirement date—and these are big decisions.

Various Pension Payouts Defined

When you first learn your pension payout options, you may be a little overwhelmed by all there is to know about pensions—and all you don't know. Since the definitions of key terms are too often muted, I've provided some standard ones and their definitions below. Most of these terms apply to both public and private pensions. You will want to consider how each of these options will affect not only you, but also your spouse or heirs when you are no longer alive. Unfortunately—as I've said before—if people knew how long they'll live, retirement planning would be so much simpler. Since none of us know, part of retirement planning is planning for the uncertainty. That's why you'll benefit from understanding these terms as you consider your make-it-within-90-days decision.

Single Life Income is typically a benefit for *only* the worker, and it is the highest monthly benefit the pension offers. The company pays this until the employee passes. Once the employee passes, whenever that is, *no* benefit remains. I have walked into many unfortunate situations where the retiree has already chosen this benefit, not knowing the risk they have subjected their spouse to. Remember, many times the retired employee has only 90 days to make the decision and has simply looked at the highest monthly benefit not knowing the ramifications of this choice in the worst-case scenario of his/her passing before the spouse does.

The *100% Joint and Survivor Benefit* will pay the *same* full benefit as long as at least one of the two are alive. If the retiree passes, the widow will receive the exact same monthly income. The survivor will then continue to receive that same benefit for the remainder of his/her life.

The *75% Joint and Survivor Benefit* option means the full pension is paid to the employee until his/her passing. After that, the survivor will receive 75% of the initial benefit.

Like the two survivor benefits above, the *50% Joint and Survivor Benefit* option means the full pension is paid to the employee until his/her passing. After that, the survivor will receive 50% of that benefit.

The *5-Year Certain,* contrary to the name, is a lifetime benefit for the retired employee. If, however, the employee passes away within the first five years of the election, the survivor will receive the remaining payments only until that initial 5-year period is complete. Then all payments stop.

The *10-Year Certain* option offers a lifetime benefit for the employee. If the employee passes away within the first 10 years, the monthly income will be guaranteed to the survivor until that initial 10-year period is complete.

A *Pop-Up Provision* is sometimes offered in a public pension plan. Attached to a joint-and-survivor option, this provision simply means that if the elected beneficiary of the joint option passes before the retired employee does, the retiree's pension will pop up to a larger amount (usually equal to the single-life option).

If you will be receiving a pension, have your financial advisor run models of the options above to figure out which course of action is best for you. If a potential retiree is not in good health, taking the lump sum may make sense: it enables that person to leave some money to the kids in a few years. If that retiree doesn't need the pension money each month, rolling the lump sum into an IRA and taking money as needed can reduce taxes. For people who have no beneficiaries and who like the idea of having a fixed income for life, the lifetime pension may be the best option. The best choice for you depends on your situation.

Like Social Security, pensions are a puzzle, and everyone is putting together a different puzzle. I cannot say this enough: You cannot just copy what your co-workers, your neighbors, or your siblings are doing. Every decision has benefits and drawbacks, so you need to weigh the options carefully, not only for you but for your heirs as well.

Income Annuities

Retirees have one other way to create lifetime income, and that is to purchase an income annuity issued by an insurance company. The monthly income amount is based on the amount of money invested in the annuity and the age at which the income will start. This income can start at retirement, before retirement, or long after retirement has begun. Some annuities are fixed; some are variable. Some annuities offer a return of partial principal if the retiree passes away early in the income stage, and some will pay a higher benefit knowing that when the owner of the annuity passes away, there will be no lump sum death benefit for his/her heirs.

You need to carefully weigh the various characteristics of the annuities you're considering. After all, the insurance company will be on the hook if you live to be 110 just as a public pension, a private pension, and Social Security will be. Insurance companies definitely build in these costs to cover that risk. If you think you'll be living long into your 90s, this option may be a good choice for at least a part of your income stream.

* * * * *

Throughout this chapter we've looked at both private and public pension plans as well as the advantages retirees have with this option. However, decisions that retirees make often come with significant risk. If you are married and/or have heirs to think about, you'll want to keep their well-being as well as your own in mind as you weigh these decisions. No simple answer to these questions about pensions and income annuities exists. Please take the time to consider each of these options carefully. I can't remind you often enough: *these decisions are irrevocable.*

* * * * *

Retirement planning is all about controlling not only today's risks, but also those risks that will arise in 20 years and along the way. Experienced financial advisors have valuable knowledge and wisdom about long-term factors in investments, so they can help you keep your retirement income flowing.

CHAPTER 8

Required Minimum Distributions

When Do You Have to Take Out RMDs?

First, **what** is a required minimum distribution (RMD)? Every qualified account acquired through an employer retirement plan and every Individual Retirement Accounts (IRAs) will have a minimum amount that you are required to withdraw every year once you hit a certain age. What is that age?

When do required minimum distributions begin? The passage of the Secure Act in 2020 moved the required minimum distributions from age 70 ½ to age 72. With the passage of the Secure Act 2.0, that age was pushed to between 73 and 75. So, depending on your date of birth, you are either already taking required minimum distributions, or you will be sometime between the ages of 72 and 75.

Secure Act 2.0 increased the age at which many of the working population would be forced to start withdrawing money from one or more of their retirement accounts. The percentage of that account value gradually increases each year according to your age. We can assume Congress raised the age for a variety of reasons: American retirees are living longer, the Social Security system needs to be adjusted, and, as I mentioned in an earlier chapter, pension plans are becoming scarcer. American employees therefore need to take greater responsibility for saving for their own comfortable retirement.

* * * * *

Back to our discussion of RMDs. If you are still employed at your RMD age and you have a retirement plan from *that* employer, **you are not required to take your minimum distributions out of that employer's retirement account.** Even if you only work a few hours a year, if you're still on the payroll and are still receiving a W-2, you don't have to take your required minimum distributions from your employer's retirement account. You will, however, need to address RMDs for your IRAs or retirement accounts *not* associated with your current employer.

So how much do you have to take out? Look at the IRS Uniform Lifetime Table on the next page. If your RMD is scheduled to begin at age 72, your first year shows a factor of 27.4. That number means that the IRS assumes you'll live for another 27.4 years. To determine your RMD, you calculate the total assets in your qualified accounts as of the previous year's 12/31 date and then divide that number by 27.4. That dollar amount is your required minimum distribution for that year: you are required to withdraw that amount from your retirement accounts sometime that calendar year. (Later in the chapter I'll address the payment frequency and from which account to withdraw your RMD.)

To look at the math another way, we can convert that 27.4 to 3.65%. Multiplying the amount of your total assets by 3.65% gives you the RMD amount you need to take out. Each year, *both* the factor *and* the corresponding conversion rate change. For instance, at age 73, you will need to withdraw slightly more as your factor decreases from 27.4 to 26.5. This change means your annual withdrawal rate increases from 3.65% to 3.78% and then to 3.93% the following year.

RMDs pose a real challenge for people choosing to have all their retirement funds in money market or fixed accounts earning 3% or less. If, for instance, the IRS forces an RMD of 3.65% and you're earning 3%, your retirement assets will drop that year by .65%. As the RMD increases the next year and in subsequent years, the IRS will be forcing you to withdraw more and more from your retirement accounts (3.78%, 3.93%, and so on). It is difficult to maintain the balance you had in the account when you first started making withdrawals. Even though it's staying invested at a stable value, your retirement savings account is snowballing downward as you are forced to withdraw more money each year than you are earning in interest. If you have any money left in your IRAs when you're 90, you'll be forced to withdraw a whopping 8.2% from your account. At this point, it becomes very difficult to earn the amount of interest/growth on your retirement accounts that you need to maintain that consistent balance.

Required Minimum Distribution

(as a percentage of assets)
*Based on Information Provided to Us

Client: _____ Date of Birth: _____

Age	Tax Year	Distribution Period	% of 12/31 Assets	12/31 Value of Qualified Plan	RMD	Date Taken
70		29.1	3.44			
71		28.2	3.55			
72		27.4	3.65			
73		26.5	3.78			
74		25.5	3.93			
75		24.6	4.07			
76		23.7	4.22			
77		22.9	4.37			
78		22	4.55			
79		21.1	4.74			
80		20.2	4.96			
81		19.4	5.16			
82		18.5	5.41			
83		17.7	5.65			
84		16.8	5.96			
85		16	6.25			
86		15.2	6.58			
87		14.4	6.95			
88		13.7	7.30			
89		12.9	7.76			
90		12.2	8.20			
91		11.5	8.70			
92		10.8	9.26			
93		10.1	9.91			
94		9.5	10.53			
95		8.9	11.24			
96		8.4	11.91			
97		7.8	12.83			
98		7.3	13.70			
99		6.8	14.71			
100		6.4	15.63			

How the Bucket Approach Can Help

If you're counting on your retirement money to last long into your 80s, the reality of the forced RMDs becomes daunting as you try to preserve your retirement accounts for your golden years. If you're planning to use retirement savings into your 80s, you may find it necessary to consider the possibility of saving in non-money-market-type investments. We believe, based on how much risk you are willing to take on, we have a solution that will help.

This approach requires you to split your retirement savings into a few different buckets of investments, specifically into at least three IRAs with different levels of risk or potential growth. This approach will work for all your IRA accounts. For illustration purposes, let's assume your first bucket is made up of primarily money market or stable value investments, and your third bucket is 100% invested in equity (or stock) investments. The second bucket is some combination of the two. If the equity market is down, you don't really want to pull RMDs from this down investment and have the double hit of a negative return on the investment *and* the withdrawal. You would reduce this account more than you intended to. So, instead, you'll take your RMDs for that year out of the safer account, your conservative bucket (or Bucket 1), while you allow the longer-term, more aggressive investments a chance to grow back.

This strategy allows you much more flexibility as you satisfy the government mandated withdrawals. If your equity investments are having a particularly good year, you may consider taking at least a part of your RMD from the equity-based portfolio. You are, in fact, taking some of the gains you experienced from the aggressive accounts and allowing your safer accounts to stay safe.

You may think that you should be more conservative with your money in retirement. You may believe that you need to get out of stocks and put everything into bonds and fixed accounts. This was the thought process several years ago when retirees were not living past 75. Today the strategy is different because we are living longer now, and our money needs to grow so that it will be there as long as we're still here. So your goal should be to earn at least an average of 4.5% annually. Depending on how much liquidity you need and your risk tolerance, you may find it possible to earn more. In addition to your risk tolerance, how much you need to withdraw at different stages of your retirement life will affect that goal.

To work on that 4.5% goal, split your IRA investments into three or four different buckets: you'll have one conservative bucket and one aggressive bucket, and the other bucket(s) will be middle-of-the-road. You'll choose which bucket to pull your RMDs from based on how the market's doing that year. This method is a plan for trying to make your money last for the rest of your life.

If you decide to leave your money in a savings account, a life span model, or one single type of investment mix, instead of using a bucket approach with different levels of risk, you'll be forced to withdraw your RMDs from that one account which may be equity-based and could be down or from that savings-based investment that would not have market risk. Whichever you chose, you would lower your portfolio more each year as your RMD amount increases every year.

How to Take Out RMDs

Perhaps you have multiple retirement plans from different employers and/or various IRA accounts. Let's say, for instance, that you have a 401k, a 403b, an IRA, and a 457. Each one of these needs to have their RMDs addressed separately. In other words, being different kinds of investment vehicles, each account will be subject to its own RMD. We have encountered many professionals, including some accountants, who are not aware of this particular rule. Many of these people seem to have thought you could simply add the values in these qualified accounts and calculate *one* single RMD amount. But if you withdraw your RMD from the 401k but do nothing with the 403b, IRA, and 457, this could be a problem.

Alternatively, say you have three IRAs, and your RMD for the year across all three IRAs is a combined $20,000 or $200,000. You can take the entire RMD from just one of the accounts, a third from each, or some from all three in any combination you want. *You* have control over the timing of your withdrawal and which account you wish to use.

Let's look at an example. Let's assume the following IRA account values as of 12/31 of the previous year, and Ms. Retiree is 75 years old.

IRA 1 *invested in a safe, fixed, stable value or money market account; liquid*	$220,000
IRA 2 *invested in an account with a combination of stocks and bonds; liquid*	$260,000
IRA 3 *a fixed-interest rate annuity with a 5-year surrender charge*	$180,000
IRA 4 *invested in an all-stock portfolio; very aggressive; liquid*	$160,000
Total IRA Value	$820,000

Based on the $820,000 total value and a factor of 4.07%, Ms. Retiree has a total RMD this year of $33,374. We know she can't take from the annuity with a 5-year surrender charge. But she invested there because interest rates were up, and wanted to lock in a very competitive interest rate for 5 years. But she has three other accounts that are liquid. If the aggressive account (IRA 4) was up 15% for the year, it gained $24,000. She could take all or some of the required $33,374 from that account. But what if the equity market has had a very hard time this year? Then her total RMD could come from IRA 1. Do you see how the power of having four differently invested IRAs can help to control how you withdraw your *forced* income?

If you have multiple different retirement plans (403b, 401k, 457), you must address these required minimum distributions separately. Doing so can be a confusing and challenging endeavor.

Once you know your RMD amount and from which account(s) you are going to withdraw the money, you will want to determine the timing and frequency of the withdrawals. You do need to take your required amount in that given year, but you have several options for how to do this. If you need monthly income, you can set up a direct deposit from an IRA or two into your bank account as a type of paycheck replacement. Again, I would schedule these for different times of the month. Or if you don't necessarily need the money, you can take a lump sum at the beginning or end of the calendar year. Some people take their lump sum at the beginning of the year to help with the property tax bill. Others prefer to let the money grow during the year and then have an early December withdrawal to help with holiday gifts.

If you truly don't need the money and would rather keep it invested, you could open an after-tax investment account. These investors choose to have the RMD money taken directly from their IRA, have a certain amount of taxes automatically withheld, and then re-invest the remaining RMD withdrawal directly into the after-tax account. These transactions are done without the retiree taking actual receipt of the money. Again, if you don't need the money, this after-tax investment has many advantages. This investment is especially advantageous if you're taking the RMD from an investment account that is down and you turn around and invest it at the same risk level. You've taken out the taxes but maintained the same type of investment that you can use later or, when you pass, leave for your heirs in a more favorable investment.

Again, the timing and method of receiving the lump sum is up to you, but the required minimum distributions must be taken by the end of the year. The only exception to this end-of-the-year rule is the year you reach RMD age: that year you have until April 1 of the following year to satisfy your RMD. If you wait, though, you will have to satisfy *that* year's RMD in addition to the previous year's RMD. In that one year you'd actually have *two* required minimum distributions added to your taxable income. You have flexibility, but your decision impacts when you pay your taxes.

Taxes and RMDs

Many people ask me if there's a way to avoid paying taxes on required minimum distributions. Before I address that, remember that when you made the deposit—and perhaps your employer made a deposit on your behalf—you and your employer received a tax break. In addition, these savings/investments all grew on a tax-deferred, compounded basis. Having benefited from those two tax-deferrals, you do have to pay the IRS its share of that sheltered income.

That said, there is one way to avoid paying taxes on RMDs. If you don't need the money, you are allowed to send all or part of your required minimum distributions from your IRA to your favorite charity. If you donate your required minimum distribution to charity and the money is sent *directly* from your IRA savings institution to the charity, you will not have to pay taxes on it, and you get to support a cause you believe in. This money will never even hit your tax return and will not need to be entered onto a Schedule C where your expenses are itemized. Very easy.

Again, required minimum distributions *must* be addressed. You cannot avoid doing so, ignore the mandate, or pretend otherwise. If you don't take out your required minimum distributions, you'll incur a substantial penalty imposed by the IRS on the amount you should have taken out. You either have to take the money for yourself or give it away to charity—or let the IRS have more.

The Problem with RMDs

As discussed earlier, the big problem with required minimum distributions is that you may not need this added income. Despite not needing it, you will be forced to take out the money. Furthermore, the unnecessary but added income from the RMD might force you into a higher tax bracket or a higher Medicare surcharge bracket based on your total taxable income.

Your financial planner will help you do all the projections and figure out how much monthly income you need. If you don't need the required minimum distribution but are forced to take it, work with your planner to figure out what to do with it. Do you invest it in a nonqualified account for the kids? Do you buy life insurance for the kids so they inherit that money income tax-free? Can you leverage the unwanted income into long-term care insurance? Are you able to create a legacy in some way?

If You Don't Need the Money...

You may want to leave your required minimum distribution money to your heirs. Unfortunately, there's a catch.

In the old days—prior to the Secure Act—if the kids inherited an IRA, they had their own required minimum distributions from that IRA, but they could spread these minimum amounts over their life. If, say, a 40-year-old inherited his 75-year-old mother's IRA of a million dollars, he could spread that money over his life expectancy (40 or more years), take out the minimum amount based on his life expectancy, and let it continue to grow. That minimum could be maybe 1.5% of the account value to begin with. Those were the good old days.

Since then, the government has giveth and taketh away. Yes, Uncle Sam increased the required minimum distribution age from 72 to 75. That was the good news. But in that same bill, Uncle Sam decided that non-spousal IRA beneficiaries now have only 10 years after the death of the IRA owner to withdraw *all* the money from that inherited IRA account.

Your 50-year-old daughter might be in her peak earning years when you pass away, and the IRA she inherits with its forced distribution may push her into a higher tax bracket. The taxes she pays on the distribution will be based on *her* earned income and the tax bracket she is in. Depending on the then-current income taxes, she could lose 30% to 45% or more of the inheritance to federal and state taxes. Again, these unavoidable income taxes will most likely be paid during her highest earning years. Although you had hoped to leave your retirement assets to your kids, you ended up leaving 30% to 45% to the government. With careful planning, you can avoid this frustrating outcome.

If you're healthy enough to get life insurance, for instance, you might be better off putting your RMDs into a life insurance policy that will benefit your heirs. This strategy repositions your taxable inheritance into a tax-free inheritance for your children and grandchildren.

I've also had clients create joint lifetime income annuities that can grow and that they can leave to their children. The retiree purchases an annuity that would provide an income for the rest of their life, and when they pass, the income continues to their beneficiary. Please be sure to speak to a fiduciary-based financial planner before considering this. That CFP® can help you look at both the positive and negative aspects of this option.

Finally, you can also put a portion of your retirement assets into a qualified longevity annuity contract (QLAC). Doing so allows you to remove the amount of that portion from your current RMD calculation, and you won't have to address required minimum distributions on that deposit until you are age 85.

Clearly, options for reducing taxes and/or creating a legacy do exist. The key is having a conversation with an experienced professional who can help you weigh the pros and cons of each approach. Addressing your RMD questions and decisions will be one of the most important discussions you'll have with your financial advisor. A mistake made here can greatly impact your heirs and their inheritances or result in your paying penalties to the IRS. Neither of those options is good. Make plans with the input or help of a financial advisor so you can avoid them both.

CHAPTER 9

Investments Before & During Retirement

Revisiting the Three-Bucket Approach

You aren't alone if investments in variables or in the equity market make you nervous. Know that having an experienced financial planner alongside you will take away much of that anxiety. When this person helps you set up your investments, you'll sleep easier at night. With a professional offering good counsel and solid guidance, you won't have to worry about whether the market is up or down and how it will affect your ability to pay the mortgage or put food on the table that month or year.

As uneasy as you are about investing, investments are necessary to sustain you and your spouse throughout your retirement years. Investing in the equity market is one of the best ways to beat inflation, but you shouldn't place your entire retirement savings in that single vehicle.

Before you retired, you were probably saving part of each paycheck automatically. With that regular savings, you were making at least a partial investment in the equity market. You may have been vaguely aware of the market being up or down, but you didn't pay much attention to it. You never even got close to panicking because you knew you wouldn't need that money until retirement. So you kept plugging away and putting your money into that equity/bond investment. By doing so, you were taking advantage of what's called *dollar-cost averaging* (see chapter 4). You invested a fixed amount on a regular basis regardless of what the market was doing. You were able to purchase more units when the market was down and fewer units when the market shares increased in price.

So what happens when you retire and instead of saving, you're pulling money out? What happens when the market drops by 10% and you're pulling out 2%? You just reduced the value of your portfolio by 12%. If you look at that drop over thirty years of returns, you're losing a lot of money, and it may be tough to make back that decrease of 12%. You can help reduce this risk of a big loss by taking a bucket approach to your retirement savings. If done correctly, this approach reduces the probability that you'll have to take money out of your stock investments in a down market.

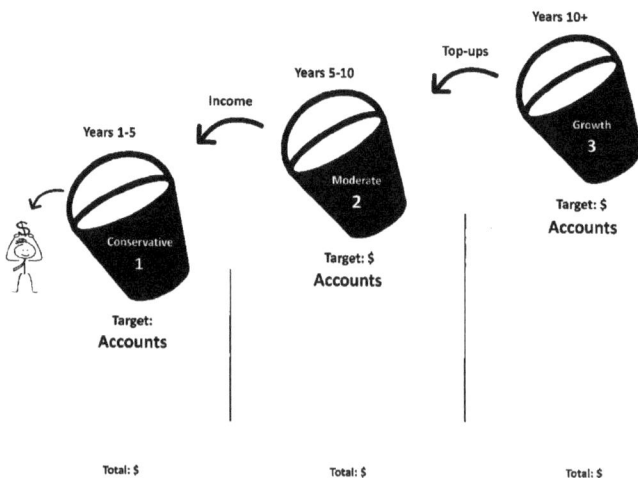

In the bucket approach, you create three buckets of money that have varying levels of investment risk. The first is the **Safe Bucket (or Bucket 1)**, and it will serve as an income source for the first 1 to 5 years of your retirement. The initial planning step is to figure out how much income you'll need for the first 1 to 5 years of retirement. Once you have that total income number, you'll calculate how much of a gap there is between your expenses and your fixed income streams, rental income, Social Security, and pensions. Then you can build the Safe Bucket to cover that gap for 1 to 5 years. If you haven't yet turned on your Social Security, you may need a little more in this first bucket compared to later buckets when Social Security payments have started.

As an example, let's assume your gap is $1,500 a month. That's $18,000 per year or $90,000 over five years. Therefore, you may need to put $75,000 to $100,000 in the first bucket, the Safe Bucket. This big bucket will sit in either the bank, a high-interest-earning money market, or a stable value type of account. The main priority is safety and liquidity. You'll have to be OK with the fact that this money isn't earning as much as it might elsewhere, but this bucket is the source of your income for your first 1 to 5 years of retirement. As part of your paycheck replacement, this Bucket #1 money is not invested aggressively, so the volatility will be much less or perhaps even nonexistent.

Bucket #2 is the **Mid-Term Bucket**, and it provides the income you'll need in 5 to 10 or 15 years into retirement. You can be a little more aggressive with this money than with the funds in the Safe Bucket. This account needs more growth, and you'll be as aggressive as you're comfortable being, knowing that you won't be using this bucket for at least 5 years from now and that it will be drawn out over a 5- or 10-year period. Depending on your risk tolerance, your aggressive investing might be 30% or 70% aggressive high-growth investments. For most people, I recommend investing 40% to 60% of their Mid-Term Bucket money in high-growth equity investments. Markets go through cycles on average every three to seven years, so money in this bucket should extend through a full cycle to allow time for a rebound in values.

The third bucket—the **Long-Term Bucket**—will provide the income you need in 10 or even 15 years into retirement and beyond, so you can be very aggressive with it, the goal being that you beat inflation. You know you won't need money from this account for several years. Of course the statements tracking these Bucket #3 accounts will look scary whenever the market takes a downturn. But if the market's doing badly and you see negatives, remind yourself that you don't need to worry because this is money for 15 years down the line. If you're seeing negatives now, remember the big picture. Know that in 15 years we should be positive again. The equity market may be down 1, 2, 3, or 5 years, for instance, but you have time to let it work its way back up. If we can trust history, we know that if we leave investments as-is over a 10- to 15-year period—if we make no emotions-based moves during that time period—we will see a positive return on our initial investment.

In addition to helping you to beat inflation, this money will probably also be used to cover some long-term care expenses should you need it. Finally, you may also be earmarking these Bucket #3 assets to leave for your heirs.

Again, you may never need this money. It may end up going to your kids. If that's the plan or the highly likely possibility, your risk tolerance changes from the timeline of a 65-year-old retiree to that of a, for instance, 40-year-old son or daughter. I have 85-year-old clients who have more than they need for their personal well-being. Realizing they have money for their children or grandchildren, they have stepped out of their comfort zone and invested it more aggressively because they have that time frame in mind. Like them, you don't have to panic if you see negatives in Bucket #3. If the market's down, you can still go on vacation, visit the grandkids, and buy Christmas gifts—you can still live life!—because this money is for 15+ years into the future.

Without this three-bucket strategy, you might constantly be worried about minimizing retirement spending and reducing retirement activities. Wouldn't it be nice to *not* worry about where your income is coming from and to get a good night's sleep even during tough economic times? A solid financial advisor and the three-bucket approach can help.

*   *   *   *   *

Now, you might have more than three buckets, and that's great. The idea here is, having investment buckets ranging from safe to aggressive gives you options as to where your income will come from. For example, some people have used fixed annuities as another Bucket #2 option in addition to the investment mix. The annuity may have a 5- to 7-year surrender charge but guaranteed high interest for those time periods.

Having these buckets set up earlier also means that you won't have to decide when to retire based on what the market is doing today or this year. Some people who don't opt for buckets that have different investment horizons end up putting off their retirement because the market is down. You want to make sure you're never in that position. It may pay what I call comfort dividends to start positioning some of your assets in a safer environment in that Bucket 1 within 3 years of a potential retirement date.

Still, the bucket approach minimizes fear and eliminates the ongoing "Should I sell or buy?" dilemma that comes with equity market investing. With the bucket approach, the markets won't dictate your life. The buckets work to protect you.

Optimizing for Maximum Income

So how do these three buckets work together? How do these different kinds of investments ensure steady and even maximum income for your retirement?

Over time, your income will continue to come primarily from the Safe Bucket #1. When you need to replenish the Safe Bucket, you'll pull money from the Mid-Term Bucket #2. Then, when the time comes, you'll use money from the Long-Term Bucket #3 to replenish the Mid-Term Bucket. The Long-Term Bucket will replenish itself over time. Again, the timing of this replenishing will be guided by several factors, including your need for income and the equity market's strength. In addition to your buckets, you will still need to have your emergency account at your bank or savings and loan, somewhere that is easily accessible and preferably doesn't create a taxable event. Also, that emergency account is liquid: you are able to draw on it for that new roof, new car engine, etc.

Again, how aggressive or conservative your bucket investing will be is based on your risk tolerance. Some people want 100% equity in the Long-Term Bucket, but some people won't go above 50%

equity. As long as you hit the target return you need for your planning, any combination of aggressive, middle-of-the-road, and conservative is OK. You're in the driver's seat. I do recommend as a goal a 4.5% return because of the eventual RMD challenge. That suggested return is based on your income needs, which you'll figure out with your financial planner.

One more note. The market goes through a complete cycle every 3 to 5 years. Every 2 years or so, you should take a look at your buckets and see if you need to make any adjustments. Maybe you've dipped into a bucket and need to replace that money. Maybe you don't need to make any adjustments. As time goes on and that 15-year mark gets closer, you'll gradually make the aggressive buckets more conservative.

It is understandably difficult to move money from a winning equity-based investment to a more conservative investment, but that kind of move needs to happen if you want to maintain this bucket approach. Whether or not, and how, to set up these buckets is one of those important Decision Decade choices. When it comes to investment decisions, the smart investor also understands the difference between greed and fear. A knowledgeable financial planner can help take the emotion out of your investments.

When to Start Building Your Buckets

You need to start building these buckets a few years before you retire. That way, a downturn in the market when you want to retire won't impact your decision.

So how do you build the buckets? You can put the money you have now into the Safe Bucket and let it grow a little bit. Many employer-sponsored retirement plans offer a stable value or a fixed account, so see if your employer does. These assets will not be invested in equity, but they usually have some type of guaranteed return. If you're not currently using this type of account, you can also start to redirect any current assets you have from stock investments into this safe bucket. It may be emotionally hard to do this when the equity market is doing well, but you absolutely need to have a plan for your next phase of life. Establishing a Safe Bucket is essential to that plan.

You need to set up this Safe Bucket at least three to five years before retirement because this is the money you're going to need right away. Again, this bucket could come through a retirement plan, or it could be a savings account. When you're close to 72, it becomes important to consider the RMD challenge of having various types of investment vehicles, and you may want to work to make all these buckets IRAs. If you do that, you'll have more flexibility when it comes time to withdraw your RMD.

Before that RMD age, it doesn't matter if your savings vehicle is a 401K, 403B, or 457. If you do have a 457, you'll probably want to deplete that first because it's owned by your employer, and you don't want to be attached to that employer once you retire. Furthermore, if that employer were to go bankrupt, you might lose immediate access to your assets, so use that money as soon as possible. Many people let their 457 account be their first source of income.

When the market is down, my friends joke with me that I must be getting a lot of calls. I do receive some, but not as many as you would guess. The reason is, clients who have worked with me to create a financial plan don't call me when the market's down because they're not worried. I've walked them through their plan many times for several years, we've discussed the nature of the investment market, and they know that a temporary dip in the market won't affect their financial security in retirement. These clients understand the buckets and where their income is coming from or will come from. The only people who call me in a panic are people who haven't set up a plan with me yet.

CHAPTER 10

Taxes

They're almost impossible to avoid, they're universally hated—and, yes I'm talking about taxes. No matter how much or how little all of us make, taxes are our common enemy. You probably think your taxes are too high, but I'm here to tell you that federal taxes are actually as low as they've ever been in history. Most of us paying income taxes have been spoiled by these low federal taxes for some time now. This relatively low rate could change especially in light of recent federal spending. We don't really know where federal taxes will be next year, much less when we retire.

It's not a surprise that taxes cause a lot of fear for people planning for their retirement. We can't predict what the tax rates will be, and you may be uncertain about what your tax bracket will be once you're not working. If you work with a financial planner, you can address some of these unknowns. Together you'll prepare your portfolio, allowing for the worst so that even if taxes do increase, you'll understand the challenge and be in better shape to work around that. Take a look at the chart on the next page for examples of the tax rate fluctuations from 1913 to 2022.

9-Feb-22

Historical Highest Marginal Income Tax Rates

Year	Top Marginal Rate	Year	Top Marginal Rate	Year	Top Marginal Rate	Year	Top Marginal Rate
1913	7.00%	1948	82.13%	1983	50.00%	2018	37.00%
1914	7.00%	1949	82.13%	1984	50.00%	2019	37.00%
1915	7.00%	1950	84.36%	1985	50.00%	2020	37.00%
1916	15.00%	1951	91.00%	1986	50.00%	2021	37.00%
1917	67.00%	1952	92.00%	1987	38.50%	2022	37.00%
1918	77.00%	1953	92.00%	1988	28.00%		
1919	73.00%	1954	91.00%	1989	28.00%		
1920	73.00%	1955	91.00%	1990	28.00%		
1921	73.00%	1956	91.00%	1991	31.00%		
1922	58.00%	1957	91.00%	1992	31.00%		
1923	43.50%	1958	91.00%	1993	39.60%		
1924	46.00%	1959	91.00%	1994	39.60%		
1925	25.00%	1960	91.00%	1995	39.60%		
1926	25.00%	1961	91.00%	1996	39.60%		
1927	25.00%	1962	91.00%	1997	39.60%		
1928	25.00%	1963	91.00%	1998	39.60%		
1929	24.00%	1964	77.00%	1999	39.60%		
1930	25.00%	1965	70.00%	2000	39.60%		
1931	25.00%	1966	70.00%	2001	39.10%		
1932	63.00%	1967	70.00%	2002	38.60%		
1933	63.00%	1968	75.25%	2003	35.00%		
1934	63.00%	1969	77.00%	2004	35.00%		
1935	63.00%	1970	71.75%	2005	35.00%		
1936	79.00%	1971	70.00%	2006	35.00%		
1937	79.00%	1972	70.00%	2007	35.00%		
1938	79.00%	1973	70.00%	2008	35.00%		
1939	79.00%	1974	70.00%	2009	35.00%		
1940	81.10%	1975	70.00%	2010	35.00%		
1941	81.00%	1976	70.00%	2011	35.00%		
1942	88.00%	1977	70.00%	2012	35.00%		
1943	88.00%	1978	70.00%	2013	39.60%		
1944	94.00%	1979	70.00%	2014	39.60%		
1945	94.00%	1980	70.00%	2015	39.60%		
1946	86.45%	1981	69.13%	2016	39.60%		
1947	86.45%	1982	50.00%	2017	39.60%		

Notes: This table contains a number of simplifications and ignores a number of factors, such as the amount of income or types of income subject to the top rates, or the value of standard and itemized deductions.

Sources: IRS Revenue Procedures, various years. Also, Eugene Steuerle, The Urban Institute; Joseph Pechman, *Federal Tax Policy*; Joint Committee on Taxation, Summary of Conference Agreement on the Jobs and Growth Tax Relief Reconciliation Act of 2003, JCX-54-03, May 22, 2003.

While you're still working, you are paying federal income taxes, state income taxes, and FICA or Social Security taxes. After you retire, you'll continue to pay federal and state taxes on your retirement plan withdrawals and your pension distributions. In addition, whether you're working or retired and depending on where you live, you may have property taxes, local taxes, and sales taxes as well.

Although you have no control over some taxes, work on what you can control. That means do what you can to reduce your federal taxes as much as possible.

State Income Taxes

As far as income taxes are concerned, not all states are created equal. Some of you might even be considering leaving your current state of residence because of state income taxes. California, for instance, has some of the highest state income taxes in the nation, with a current high marginal rate of 12.3%. A tax rate like this can be a substantial expense for some retirees and therefore must be considered during retirement planning.

Other states, however, have very low or even no state income taxes. Currently, the eight states that have no income taxes are Alaska, Florida, Nevada, South Dakota, Tennessee, Texas, Washington, and Wyoming. Obviously, you'll have to consider several other factors (including the type of income you have because not all income is taxable) before you leave for one of those eight states. If most of your income is nontaxable, whether or not a state has income taxes won't be a factor in your decision to retire to another state. But if your goal is to reduce your state income taxes in retirement, you do have some options.

Tax Diversification

Since we can't predict future tax rates at either the federal or state level, our strategy is to build flexibility into our income streams. While you're working, try not to save only in employer-sponsored retirement plans. Also, you'll want to diversify your investments to include both tax-deferred (or qualified) and nonqualified, so that you have access to different buckets of money with different tax ramifications to help you control whatever your income taxes will be.

In my practice, we use a one-page tool that helps us organize all our clients' assets whether their goal is building wealth or creating income. We call it our bubble chart, and we use it in every client meeting because it helps us understand tax implications, determine what assets should be held in their trust, and easily see what assets can be relied upon for income and which assets could be earmarked for the heirs. Some clients, in fact, keep a copy of this one page handy in the event they suddenly pass. This one-pager will give their heirs a general idea of assets, information that is especially important if they've never talked about it.

You can see the five columns. We'll focus on the Retirement and Long-Term columns.

Portfolio & Planning Overview

Core Assets
Date

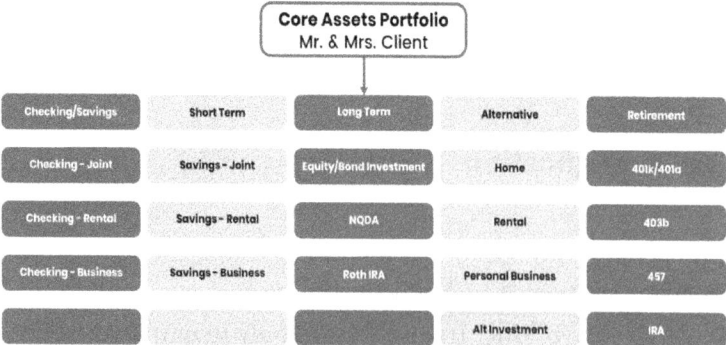

Core Assets Portfolio
Mr. & Mrs. Client

Checking/Savings	Short Term	Long Term	Alternative	Retirement
Checking - Joint	Savings - Joint	Equity/Bond Investment	Home	401k/401a
Checking - Rental	Savings - Rental	NQDA	Rental	403b
Checking - Business	Savings - Business	Roth IRA	Personal Business	457
			Alt Investment	IRA

The right-hand column on the bubble chart—the Retirement column—lists different types of **qualified money**, investments like the typical 401k, a 403b plan, a 457 plan as well as IRA accounts and the RMDs associated with them. This column includes any investment that offers a tax break when you deposit the money into the account. You will pay income taxes when you take the money out of the account.

401k plans are the most well-known employer-sponsored plans. Although some exceptions exist, 401k plans are typically available to employees of for-profit organizations. These plans create ordinary income at distribution, not capital gains.

403b plans are similar to a 401k, but they are for employees of nonprofit organizations like schools, churches, and hospitals.

Usually governmental retirement savings plans, **457 plans** are common for city and county employees like police and firefighters. The 457 is different because it is a deferred compensation plan: the government agency actually owns the money, and it is held on their books until you are retired and start to withdraw that money. If the government agency goes bankrupt or has financial trouble, your money may be frozen and inaccessible until the agency works through their bankruptcy. (This happened several years ago here in Orange County, California. I don't think anyone lost any 457 funds, but those funds were inaccessible for a period.) Because of this risk, we often advise clients to use their 457 monies as the first bucket of money if a strong, safe interest-rate account is available or to move those monies into an IRA outside of their employer's control as soon as possible. Depending on the type of 457, however, employees may not be allowed to roll their plan into an IRA. They might be required to take it in the form of income.

* * * * *

We're also going to look at the middle column which lists Long-Term sources of money. This column includes annuities and simple after-tax investments. With nonqualified deferred annuities (**NQDA**), you usually put a lump sum of money in after-tax, and it grows tax deferred. In fact, the primary purpose of NQDA is to defer the taxes on that investment until a later date. Some people have used NQDA to eventually build an income stream. You can't withdraw this NQDA money before age 59 ½. When you do decide to withdraw, it's LIFO (Last In, First Out): you will first take out the taxable income before you access the money that you initially deposited. Again, income from the NQDA is considered regular income and is therefore taxable. Because of that interest being forced out first (LIFO), this income—although not required to be withdrawn—is taxed similarly to the way that your retirement accounts will be taxed when you start taking the money out. You'll want to carefully review these options with a professional so you understand the kind of access you'll have to your money.

If you currently have a large employment income, you may deposit money in a nonqualified investment such as a simple brokerage account, a mutual fund, or individual stocks. Each year, you'll receive a 1099, and that means you'll pay regular income taxes on those dividends even if you don't take receipt of the dividends and instead choose to have them re-invested. Each year those taxed dividends add to your original cost basis. This allows you to not pay tax on dividends *twice* when you sell the asset.

Capital gains taxes are paid only when you sell the securities, and capital gains taxes may be less than income taxes. Depending on how capital gains taxes compare to income taxes, having money in both qualified and nonqualified investments will give you more tax flexibility.

You might have a blended 401k plan where the 401k is made up of both pre-tax and after-tax money. You, the employee, may have deposited money after taxes, and your employer matched you with pre-tax money. Without talking to an advisor when you retire, you might move the whole thing into an IRA because you wouldn't know any better. Moving the entire balance into an IRA would be a mistake because you'd pay double taxes on your after-tax money.

Tax-Free Retirement Income Using Roth Accounts

We've discussed different types of accounts that have different types of taxes due on the withdrawals, but wouldn't it be great to have a stream of tax-free income in retirement? The **Roth retirement accounts**—Roth IRA, Roth 401k, Roth 403b, and Roth 457— allow you to enjoy tax-free income during your retirement. Since 2006, employers have been allowed to amend their provided retirement plans to allow for Roth-type contributions. This amendment allows many people who might not typically be eligible for a Roth IRA contribution the opportunity to use this unique tool. I would strongly encourage you to ask your employer if this type of benefit is available.

You'll also need to decide what's more important to you, reducing your "later" tax rates or reducing the tax burden for your heirs. Once you go through various models with your financial planner and make sure you have enough money to last through your lifetime, you'll start the process of deciding which assets to leave to your heirs. Remember, when you pass, these Roth accounts go to your heirs *tax-free.*

The most tax-efficient assets to leave to your heirs are Roth IRAs as well as nonqualified assets and real property. If you leave nonqualified assets to your heirs, they will have the opportunity for a stepped-up basis, meaning your heirs would assume the date-of-death value of the investment as their own basis. It will be as if they themselves made the investment, so they avoid all the taxes on the difference between the original investment plus the reinvested dividends *and* that day-of-death value, the amount the investment grew. If titled correctly, this stepped-up basis makes nonqualified assets one of the most efficient assets to leave to the children.

In sharp contrast, qualified money is the worst asset for your heirs to inherit because someone, somewhere, will sometime have to pay the income taxes due on all this deferred income. Let's say you and your spouse pass away and leave your children and/ or grandchildren all your IRA assets. Based on the most recent changes in tax law, your kids will have 10 years to take the entire balance out. If you end up passing in your 80s, your kids are probably in their 50s, their peak earning years. Their tax bracket is already high, and now you've left them an IRA that bumps them into an even higher bracket. They might lose 50% of their IRA inheritance to taxes. Talk to a financial advisor about how to avoid this awful scenario.

Again, you need to assess your financial situation and figure out your top priority: reducing your own taxes or reducing your heirs' taxes. Your answer will determine which investments you pull money from and at what pace you pull it. Everyone's situation is unique, making this another Decision Decade choice impacted by both your personal financial situation and your heirs' economic circumstances.

Roth Conversions

If federal income taxes are historically low right now, would you expect them to increase or drop further before you retire? If you expect an increase, why wouldn't you prepare for it? Why wouldn't you do what you can to avoid that extra taxable income? To take action now, look into a **Roth conversion**, which is simply the process of moving money from a tax-deferred retirement account, such as a traditional IRA, into a Roth IRA. Contrary to what you may think, there is no earned income limit on how much you can convert.

To convert to a Roth, you will take some or all of the money from your traditional IRA account, pay the current income tax on that amount, and then move to a new Roth IRA. Once you've done this Roth conversion, your money will grow tax deferred. At your RMD age, you will not be required to take that forced distribution. An immediate advantage to this conversion is that it doesn't affect your taxable income or your possible Medicare surcharge.

A Roth conversion does have a downside, though. In the year you finish the conversion, you will need to add to your taxable income the amount you converted. You'll pay those taxes using funds in your savings account, not your Roth conversion assets. You will need to have funds readily available to cover the taxes.

* * * * *

You may have picked up on the fact that you don't have to do a Roth conversion all at once. You can convert a smaller amount each year, an amount that lets you avoid a Medicare surcharge and keeps you under the next tax bracket.

If you're a rather aggressive investor, Roth conversions make more sense when the market's down and/or you have experienced a drop in income. If you believe that the equity markets are going to rebound in the long-term, why wouldn't you take that IRA value, convert it to a Roth, pay the income taxes on that amount, and ride that growth back up in a tax-deferred and eventually tax-free investment? For example, assume you have a $200,000 IRA invested in the S&P 500 index fund. The S&P 500 is down 25% this year, but you still believe the S&P 500 is, over the long term, a great place to keep your retirement funds. Your account value is now $150,000 because it has lost 25%. So convert the $150,000 (instead of the $200,000) to a Roth. You'll pay taxes on $150k rather than on $200k in the conversion. As that $150k grows back to $200k, that growth and the eventual withdrawal will be tax free.

When you withdraw money from a Roth IRA, all the growth is now tax-free. We have clients converting their money into a Roth so that their two-year-old grandson will have money for college. A Roth IRA is basically another way to build a tax-free college savings plan that is *not* tied to going to college. Your grandchildren could use it to pay for a wedding or their first home, or you could keep it for yourself.

* * * * *

When you do a Roth conversion, you don't have to sell the stocks that your money is invested in. Your assets will just transfer into the Roth. A 401k works a little differently. You can't convert a 401k or 403b directly to a Roth IRA. You first must move the 401k into an IRA and then convert that IRA to a Roth IRA.

Once your money is in the Roth, it grows tax-deferred, and you can take it out tax-free at your convenience. You'll never be forced to take it out via required minimum distributions. When you pass away, the Roth IRA goes to your heirs tax-free. One caveat about that: your heirs are still required to withdraw the entire amount within 10 years, but it won't taxed and therefore won't affect their income tax level.

Other Ways to Reduce Your Tax Burden in Retirement

If a Roth conversion is not an option, a second way to reduce your tax burden in retirement is to **take out more money from your taxable accounts now**, on a monthly basis, even though you're not required to and may not need it. You'll pay the current income tax rate on this money now and then invest it in nonqualified assets where you'll have dividends and capital gains, and your heirs will be able to take advantage of the stepped-up basis upon your death.

Yes, you're depleting your qualified money sooner rather than later even though you don't need it. But you're moving this money from one bucket to another as an investment vehicle and paying taxes while the tax brackets are still lower than you believe they will eventually be. If you never need the money, your heirs will have a stepped-up cost basis, and the taxes due should be less.

A third option for reducing your tax burden is **donating all or a portion of your RMD to charity**. Most people donate to their particular nonprofit entities by writing a check and then deducting that amount from their income taxes through a Schedule C. They may do this annually or monthly. If you have RMDs that you don't need as income, though, you can have your annual donation to the charity come directly from your IRA in the tax year the RMD is required. Doing so is considered a qualified charitable contribution.

Finally, let me set the stage for a fourth option. Let's say you're retiring with a large enough monthly pension that you don't need the qualified assets in your 457 account or IRA that you worked hard to save. You aren't yet 72 years old, but you know that you'll eventually be required to take this money. This additional income will no doubt place you in a higher tax bracket. So consider **an asset transfer from a qualified account to a real property**. Purchasing a second home or a vacation home will transfer taxable income to a nonqualified asset that can be more tax efficient when you pass. Take money out of your 457 plan each month to pay the mortgage. In addition to transferring assets to a different asset class (retirement account to real property), you'll have a place where you can vacation with your kids and grandkids. You're putting your money to good use while you're alive, and you can leave the house as a tax-efficient asset to your heirs when you pass away.

CHAPTER 11

Estate Planning

Do you have a living trust? That's one of the first questions I ask people when they sit down with me to plan for retirement.

If you only have qualified accounts and you rent your home, you probably won't need a trust. Your qualified accounts are beneficiary-designated accounts, so they will already be passed on to your kids or whomever you name as your beneficiary.

But if you own a house, have nonqualified investments, have a certain amount of money sitting in the bank, or have confusing inheritance issues because you've blended two families into one, you will **need a living trust for clarity and to avoid probate**. The threshold varies by state, but in California, if you have assets outside of a trust and a nonbeneficiary designated account with a value of more than $150,000, probate will open. If you pass away without a living trust and probate opens, settling your estate will be time-consuming and expensive for your heirs.

* * * * *

Have you put off establishing a living trust because you're worried about **paying an attorney**? For a simple living trust, an attorney may charge $1500 to $5500. In contrast, probate will cost approximately 3% to 6% of your *total* estate. The value of your estate includes the value of your home even if you have an outstanding mortgage. With a home and invested assets, your estate can easily total $1M or more. The probate range of 3% to 6% would mean an unnecessary and avoidable expense of $30,000 to $60,000 on a $1M estate.

Furthermore, your estate will sit in probate court for 12 to 18 months. If your children want to sell your home after you pass, they won't be able to until it has gone through probate. Since you didn't have a trust, you didn't designate anyone as your sole beneficiary, so the courts will have to determine the actual beneficiary who's entitled to that house. That investigation will mean additional costs and a delay in closing your estate, both of which could have been avoided. You need a living trust.

*   *   *   *   *

Still not convinced? Living trusts also **protect you from creditors**. What happens if you're driving but don't see the person in the crosswalk, and you hit that person? If your assets aren't held inside of a trust, they're liable to any creditor. In the scenario I just described, you could be sued and lose much of your saved assets. But if you have a living trust and your assets are held in the trust, those assets will be protected in cases like the above example.

*   *   *   *   *

I do understand why people want to avoid setting up a living trust: people don't want to face their mortality. It can be uncomfortable to think about and talk about your death. But if you die without a living trust, the situation is scarier and more painful for your family. Even though you may feel strange and awkward sitting down with an attorney and talking about your own death, it's a necessary process if you want to protect your assets for your loved ones. And you shouldn't wait until you are five years retired. When I established the first version of our family's trust, I was 33 years old. Why wait?

What Is a Trust?

A trust is a legal document that records where you want your assets to go after you pass away.

A trust is different from a will. A will lists your *wishes* regarding the distribution of your assets. It says what you want to do, but there's no provision for these wishes being fulfilled. On the other hand, a trust records your wishes *and* establishes a third party to direct the assets. The main and perhaps most important difference is that **a will does not avoid probate** whereas a living trust, by federal law, does.

One document included in a living trust is your **durable powers of attorney**: you designate someone to make decisions for you if you're incapacitated. There will be two sets of durable powers. One will cover your finances, one will cover your health care—and these powers do not need to be given to the same person. If you get sick and are unable to make decisions, you may need your spouse to manage your finances, and a durable power of attorney will allow that to happen. Similarly, a health care directive will allow the person you designate to make decisions about your health care if you are unable to.

Many people think that if you set up a living trust and transfer your assets into your trust, you lose control over those assets. That's not true. While you're alive, you're the trustee of your own trust. You'll designate a successor trustee to manage the trust after you pass away. This person will find your plans for your estate outlined in your trust and then act accordingly.

If your trust is more than 10 years old, you should have it reviewed and updated. The many changes to federal tax laws may or may not affect the design of your trust, so I strongly advise a professional review. For example, I used to have an AB trust that allows a couple, upon the first death, to split the assets of the marital party in two to help alleviate or eliminate estate taxes that may come due at that death. But then tax laws changed, and the exclusion allowance—the amount subject to estate tax upon my death—increased so much that I switched to a simple trust. After all, when I pass away, I want the trust to be very simple for my wife and children to administer.

*   *   *   *   *

For most people today, a **simple trust** may be completely adequate. With an AB trust, upon the first passing, the assets will be split into two, half allotted to the survivor and the other half to the deceased. For the deceased's share of the trust, the survivor will not only have to file for a tax ID number but also file an annual tax return for the trust every year. Those assets will not be distributed until the second death, so this could be a lot of years of filing a separate tax return for a minimal estate. With a simple trust, you can avoid these complications and make it easier for your family after you pass away.

* * * * *

I do recommend that you bring your financial advisor when you meet with an attorney to set up your trust. A financial advisor can ask the attorney questions about your family and your situation that you may not know to ask. The process can be a bit confusing and quite daunting, but an experienced financial advisor who is working on your behalf—and who is interested in your overall well-being—can help you understand the decisions you're making and, with the attorney, advise you on how to best protect your assets.

* * * * *

When you develop your financial plan, work with your planner to create a **beneficiary checklist**. You'll make a list of your retirement plans and IRA accounts and, next to each, the people you've named as beneficiaries—and be sure to keep this list of beneficiaries updated. Sometimes people don't update this list for 15 years, and they'll have ex-spouses or people who have died listed as their beneficiaries. Inaccuracies like these can create a real mess. Furthermore, if you pass away and your beneficiaries have died, you may not even have a beneficiary.

If you have no beneficiary listed, the state will decide what to do with your assets. Each state has its own process. Many states will first try to find your spouse, but the state won't know your current situation or specific wishes. The state will look for parents, children, aunts, and uncles but not consider that close friend you've had for 30 years and whom you intended to help even after you were gone.

The point is, if you don't name a beneficiary or if your beneficiary list is outdated, you're letting the state control who gets your money. We've heard too many stories of a wife who divorced her husband, remarried, but didn't change the beneficiary on her retirement account. When she passed 10 years later, the retirement plan had to be paid out to the ex-husband, whom she'd never removed as the beneficiary. Again, be sure to check your beneficiary designations every five years to confirm that you're not leaving assets to deceased people or to people you're no longer on good terms with. Not keeping your list of beneficiaries up-to-date is one of the most overlooked problems with estate planning—and one of the first areas that should be addressed.

* * * * *

You will want to do a beneficiary audit at least as often as you update your financial plan. Sometimes people will name **minors as beneficiaries** not knowing that the money will be unavailable to the minors until they are age 18 or 21, depending on the state. The better option would be to name as the beneficiary the person you are designating to take care of this minor after you pass. That adult will have immediate access to the funds.

Sometimes people will put **a trust as the primary beneficiary** of their retirement accounts, and there are pros and cons to this option. The retirement accounts will automatically be paid to the trust. Since a trust is a nonperson, it will always be taxed at the highest marginal tax bracket when these accounts are paid out at the time of your death. Despite that financial fact, some people do name a trust as a beneficiary because they don't have children, and they want the trustee to oversee the distribution of money to charities and distant relatives. This approach may make sense, but a simpler way to do that would be to set up separate IRAs and name a different charity or relative the beneficiary for each one. Then the money will go directly to the people or organization you want to leave it to without involving a middleman.

Also, know that a particular type of trust is needed if you have a disabled child, relative, or spouse who regularly receives government assistance. If you pass away and leave your government-assisted individual as a beneficiary of your trust, that government assistance might stop or be largely reduced because that individual is suddenly receiving income and assets from your trust. You can avoid this by setting up a **special needs trust** that keeps your money inside a separate trust. Then your designated trustee can direct money to your beneficiary as needed to supplement the government assistance.

*   *   *   *   *

When it comes to your estate, sometimes your **employer** has automatically enrolled you in a **retirement plan** you didn't know about. Either the employer has deposited money, or money has been automatically deducted from your paycheck and deposited into a retirement plan. With employers rarely offering pensions, these auto-enrolled plans have become more popular. You'll want to be aware of these plans on your behalf so that these investments are included in your cash flow planning and that you have named a beneficiary. You want to make sure this money goes to the right person or place.

Trust Alternatives

I'll occasionally sit down with people and see that most of their assets are in a retirement plan. They don't have much in what we call trust assets or substantial assets outside of their retirement plan. So instead of going to the trouble of setting up a living trust, I may help these people designate their nonqualified assets as a payable on death (POD) or a transfer on death (TOD) account. The term depends on the institution holding the accounts.

Naming an asset payable on death/transfer on death is like putting a beneficiary on a nonretirement plan. If you have less than $150,000 in a savings account, for instance, you can name your daughter as a beneficiary so she has immediate access to it when you pass away and can use some of the money for funeral expenses.

Life Insurance

Life insurance can either be owned by the trust, or the trust could be the beneficiary of a life insurance policy. You need to talk to a financial advisor to determine the best option for you. Most people name an individual as the beneficiary of a life insurance policy because then the life insurance proceeds are paid tax-free. There are never any taxes on life insurance when you pay it to an individual.

But let's back up. You want to have—and you need to have—life insurance for a few reasons. If your passing is going to create financial hardship for your spouse, you need to have life insurance so he/she doesn't have to worry about the debt you've left behind and the income you will not be earning for your family. If your family is relying on you to make $80,000 per year (and with inflation, we know that expected income will increase over time), what total amount will your family miss out on for the next 20 years if you aren't here? How will your not being here affect your spouse and your children and their standard of living when you are gone?

I always tell my clients that life insurance is love insurance. If you have someone you love, you need life insurance. You don't want the people you love to have their life turned completely upside down by having to find a new home, go to a new school, or start receiving government assistance. Also, if you have young kids, you might want to add a little more life insurance, so they'll have money to go to college. You want to have a financial planner help you determine the amount of life insurance to carry—and I can assure you it will be more than what your employer is providing for you.

Annuities

Investors will deposit money into annuities for one of two primary reasons: either to defer taxes on the interest or on the growth of an investment or to create an eventual income stream. Because of the advantage of sheltering future investment earnings from being taxed, annuities can be very helpful.

Annuities can also become a huge problem if they aren't correctly titled. An annuity has three participants: the annuitant, the contract owner, and the beneficiary. (A trust can own a nonqualified annuity.) You will have to clearly specify what happens if any of the three parties involved with the annuity were to pass away so that the annuity will be titled correctly. Otherwise, the annuity can lead to a very complicated situation when you die. When you set up annuities, you definitely want to work with your financial advisor and ask questions about what happens if any of the three participants were to pass away.

* * * * *

Finally, let me again acknowledge that deciding what will happen to your assets after your death can be an uncomfortable conversation. But if you make plans for your estate with a financial advisor you trust, you can protect your assets and relieve the burden on your family after you pass away. If your financial advisor is not addressing these very important issues, you might want to find a financial advisor who does.

Before You Go...

You've Read the Book. Why Not Act Now?

"I wish I'd done this sooner." These are the words I hear from clients when we complete their initial retirement plan.

Too many people spend years during their 40s and 50s wondering if they'll be able to retire. I don't want you to wonder and worry.

I want you to spend the last years of your career confident that you have a secure financial plan in place for the next phase of your life.

The moment you make your plan, your stress will disappear, and you'll wonder why you didn't get this financial planning for retirement out of the way years ago.

Benefits of Having a Retirement Plan in Place

When you have a retirement plan in place, you don't have to worry that the market is going up, down, or sideways.

You will be in control of deciding whether to hang on at work when the environment is toxic because you'll know you have enough saved.

You'll be prepared in advance for whatever financial challenges come your way.

You can stop focusing on your fears and start focusing on your dreams.

The earlier you plan, the more within reach your retirement dreams will be. Do you want to travel abroad and help your grandkids pay for college? Great, you can make that happen easily—and the sooner you start, the easier it will be.

Sadly, I've seen some people wait too long and have to give up certain goals and dreams that their finances can't sustain. They kick themselves because they could have reached those goals and realized those dreams if they'd started planning earlier.

But now that you've read this book, you know what these people didn't.

When you give yourself enough time to prepare, you will have minimized your fears and maximized the chance that you'll fulfill your dreams.

Once your financial plan for retirement is in place, you're free.

When your neighbors panic over the latest amount of money a so-called media expert says you need to save before you can retire, you can sit back and relax. You know your number.

When your co-workers wonder if they have to stay at the office another decade, you can breathe easy knowing you can leave on your terms and whenever you want.

And when your friends approach 65 and frantically pore over Social Security brochures, you and your spouse can instead pore over travel brochures for your first post-retirement vacation.

Remember, Failure Is Not an Option

You only get one shot at retirement, and running out of money before you run out of life is not a risk you want to take. Now that you've learned everything you need to know to prepare for the retirement of your dreams, what are you waiting for?

Every second you wait, you're not experiencing the confidence that can give you real peace of mind. Why not work toward that now?

Do yourself a favor and make your life easier.

You don't have to sit with your stress another year, another week, another day…

You deserve to be excited about rather than worried about your future. You've worked long and hard. It's now time for all your retirement dreams to be your reality.

If you're ready to let go of fear and embrace freedom, you know what to do. Find a financial planner and start working to build your plan together.

The first step is easy...

If you're ready to plan your retirement and you want a guide, I'd like the opportunity to speak with you. Give my office a call at (949) 341-4188 and let's talk about your options. You can also email me at mike.lockwood@lfg.com or visit our website at www. oakwoodwealthpartners.com We can chat about your goals, your needs, and your unique retirement plan. I hope this book has encouraged you and shown you all the good that is possible.

About the Author

I always want to know something about the person I'm going to for advice and help in making decisions. That's why I'm letting you know a little bit about me.

I had graduated from college. I'd earned my CERTIFIED FINANCIAL PLANNER™ certification. I knew what I knew. But in all honesty, it took a couple years as a financial planner before I really trusted my judgment and training. After all, I simply didn't have the life experience that my clients did. I could empathize as they shared with me, but I hadn't yet lived through the challenges, concerns, hopes, and fears that they had. So sometimes when I realized the significance of the decisions I was making and helping my clients to make, I was a little overwhelmed. My clients—these individuals who were entrusting me to take care of their money—relied on me and, eventually, on my team. Being able to help people like this was very gratifying, but it came with a tremendous sense of responsibility.

* * * * *

Early in my career, I was told that if you imagine yourself in the place of the people you're advising, you can't go wrong. If you were in the same specific circumstances that your client is in, what decision would you make? This approach is the basis of the CERTIFIED FINANCIAL PLANNER™ creed. But more important to me is that every individual I hire to be part of our practice has a good, caring heart and a willingness to serve people. In fact, we are here to serve our clients, and that commitment has to be at the forefront of our thoughts and actions. Serve first, last, and always, in all that we all do each and every day. The technical stuff will be learned over time. Heart can't be taught.

* * * * *

After 35 years as a CERTIFIED FINANCIAL PLANNER™ professional, I am not only confident about what I do for my clients, but I am also confident enough to bring new advisors into my fold and work with them as they learn and grow. I have found this career immensely impactful and satisfying. After all, I'm able to help shape people's lives not just for today, but also for twenty or thirty years from now when their planning will benefit their heirs and other people they care about. Countless clients have thanked me for the simple advice I gave them 25 or so years ago: every year I simply pushed them to save a little more than they had been saving. Clients I have coached over many years have become friends, and seeing the results of our planning together may be the most rewarding aspect of my calling.

* * * * *

Many times when professionals come to me, referred to me by a mutual friend, they lament not knowing how to plan for their retirement and sometimes admit to a fear of that not-yet-planned-for future. Some of these professionals do have a grasp on where they're going and how to get there, but others are completely lost. Experts in their chosen profession, they aren't comfortable dealing with such topics as CDs, mutual funds, Social Security, and Medicare. Our team's job is to assure these new friends that their uneasiness is quite common and that many people have the same questions, uncertainty, and discomfort when it comes to retirement planning.

I have said many times to my new clients who are nurses, "You handle the IVs; I'll handle the money. I wouldn't know where to begin with an IV, so don't even ask me to try!" My point is, most of us are experts at something. Financial planning is my area of expertise.

* * * * *

I have always been a hard worker. In my one-parent home, if I wanted spending money, I had to earn it, so I did. At age 13 I got my first job: I filled bags of ice at Mr. K's liquor store in Mountain View, California. I earned 50 cents every time I worked in the store no matter how much ice I needed to bag. My job was to make sure the freezer was full of bags of ice. Eventually, I moved on to other jobs: I washed dishes, pruned grapes in the winter, dried apricots in the summer, and eventually was the night manager at a Baskin-Robbins for two years.

Even before I was in high school, attending college was a goal of mine. A couple role models in my life had gone to college, and I had this crazy thought that I could do that too. So after I graduated from high school, I became the first member of my family to attend college. Having no financial assistance from my family, I knew I had to pay for my own education. I had dreams of going to a big school, but there was no way I could afford that. It did take me six years, but I graduated from California State University, Bakersfield, with a double Business Marketing and Finance degree—and a Theater minor! I worked full-time and took out several student loans to make that college dream a reality in my life.

When I graduated at age 23, Lincoln National hired me to help hospital employees save money for retirement in a 403b account. Ironically, I was encouraging others to adopt sound financial practices even though I myself had made many personal mistakes with my money along the way, but I'd always learned from those mistakes. As my life experiences started piling up, my confidence in my ability to be an effective financial planner grew.

When I think about my first position with Lincoln, I have to say it was a little crazy that this 23-year-old college graduate was visiting with 50- and 60-year-old hospital employees to encourage them to save money for retirement through equity investments.

What in the world did I know about retirement? Fortunately, I had some great mentors along the way, and I persevered.

*   *   *   *   *

Throughout my career, I have had various titles and responsibilities with Lincoln. In addition to running my own practice and building my own team, I have had the pleasure hiring and mentoring at least 25 advisors who are now working throughout Southern California. I have also helped four senior advisors retire, reassuring them that my team and I would take good care of their clients and continue to ensure their financial well-being. I have served on several national boards committed to improving the service model in our industry and to fostering the continued growth of our chosen profession. Through all of this, my wife, Michelle, and I have built our greatest legacy and my greatest source of pride: our family. Our three children—Nick, Lauren, and Grant—are now creating their own path in life.

*   *   *   *   *

I tell you all this about myself because I want you to know me. I want you to realize that I understand the challenges of paying all the bills, wondering if I can afford to put money into savings, and being concerned about having money when I need it.

After 35 years as a financial advisor and 22 years as a CFP® Professional, I am not only educationally equipped to guide others, but I am now a seasoned planner who can relate to many of the decisions and concerns that my retirees and almost-retirees face. At the same time, I remember my roots.

Again, when you hire a financial advisor or financial coach, I believe it's good for you to know what motivates them and where they have come from. Now you know my story. I'd like to hear yours.

www.ingramcontent.com/pod-product-compliance
Lightning Source LLC
Chambersburg PA
CBHW070931210326
41520CB00021B/6883